On The Door

The Geoff Thompson Story

Part Three

Geoff Thompson

SUMMERSDALE

Summersdale Publishers Ltd
46 West Street
Chichester
West Sussex
United Kingdom
PO19 1RP

Printed and bound in Great Britain by Biddles Ltd.,
Guildford and King's Lynn.

ISBN 1 84024 082 2

The names of some of the people and places in this book
have been changed to protect the guilty.

Other books and videos by Geoff Thompson:

Watch My Back - *A Bouncer's story*.

Bouncer (the sequel to **Watch My Back**)

The Pavement Arena
- *adapting combat martial arts to the street*.

Real Self Defence.

Real Grappling.

Real Punching

Real Kicking.

Weight Training For the Martial Artist.

Animal Day - *Pressure testing the martial arts*.

Tuxedo Warrior - *Tales of a Mancunian bouncer*.
By Cliff Twemlow. Foreword By Geoff Thompson.

Fear - the friend of exceptional people.
Techniques in controlling fear.

Dead or Alive - *the complete self protection handbook*
(as released by Paladin Press in the USA).

Blue Blood on the Mat
Athol Oakley - Foreword Geoff Thompson.

The Ground Fighting series:
Vol One - Pins, the bedrock.
Vol Two - Escapes.
Vol Three - Chokes and Strangles.
Vol Four - Arm bars and Locks.
Vol Five - Fighting from neutral knees.
Vol Six - Fighting from your back.

Videos - (all videos one hour approx)

Lessons with Geoff Thompson
Animal Day - *pressure testing the martial arts.*
Animal Day Part 2, *a deeper look - the fights.*

Three Second Fighter - *the sniper option.*

The Ground Fighting series
Vol One - Pins, the bedrock.
Vol Two - Escapes.
Vol Three - Chokes and strangles
Vol Four - Bars and joint locks.
Vol Five - Fighting from neutral knees.
Vol Six - Fighting from your back.

Forthcoming books:
Real Head, Knees and Elbows.
Contemporary Self Protection
(released as *Dead or Alive* in USA).

About The Author

Geoff Thompson has to be one of the most recognised and controversial martial arts writers and teachers of this century with some twenty bestselling books on the contemporary role of martial arts to his name. His work is both innovative and thought provoking. As an ambassador for the martial arts he has appeared on national and international TV and radio talking about and giving advice on self protection and related subjects. He has taught his unique method of self protection to the police, the Royal Marine Commandos, in local government, on Excel Body Guard training camps and also on the professional circuit. Geoff's first book *Watch My Back - A Bouncer's Story* (also released in the USA by Paladin Press) about his nine years working as a night club doorman is widely recognised as a cult book. His other books have also been highly successful. He now writes regular columns for several publications including: SG's *Martial Arts*, *Martial Arts Illustrated*, *Combat, Traditional Karate, Fighters*, Terry O'Neill's *Fighting Arts International, Muscle Mag* (Britain-USA), *Black Belt Magazine* (USA) *Fighters* (Sweden) and *Australasian Fighting Arts* (Australia). He has also featured in mainstream glossy magazines such as *Loaded, Maxim,* and *Esquire* and has published several articles with *GQ Magazine* (Britain-France). Geoff also has to be one of the most practised instructors of our day with a long list of combat qualifications. He is presently a Sambo Russian Wrestling Coach, Olympic Greco Roman Wrestling Coach (FILA), Olympic Free style Wrestling Coach (FILA), Ju-Jitsu coach, Judo Coach, British Combat Association Coach, EKGB 4th Dan, JKA 2nd Dan, Shoalin Modga gung fu 1st Dan, ABA, ass Boxing Coach and BTBC Muay Thai Boxing Coach. He is a former UK Weapons Champion and is trained in the use of the Defensive Flashlight and the PR24 Side Handled Baton. He has also trained in Aikido and weapons. As well as his books and videos Geoff has written 12 TV plays based on his bouncer books. Although recognised as an international authority on the art of self protection, his work in reality training is still thought of as heresy in some quarters of the martial arts world.

A Poem

- by the late Percy Rowley
(written a couple of months before he died of cancer)

Sometimes, when I'm cooking my dinner
My fingers get burnt and I shout
and then I look in the mirror
and I wonder, what life's all about?
And I wonder what waits in the future
and I think of the things in my past
and then I think of the present and
I wonder how long it can last!
I've had a good run and I'm happy
and I tried to do everything right.
I thank God when I wake in the morning
and I still say my prayers at night.
I know that I can't live forever
and I know when they lay me to rest
that I did what I could,
sometimes more than I should
but at least I did try my best?

Dedication

I would like to dedicate this book to my late and wonderful friend Percy Rowley — who was braver than I could ever be. The first one off the press is yours Perc. Also - dedicated to my old friend and colleague Eddie 'killer' Kilbane killed this year (1996) in a bar fight in Coventry. To Andy Davis' mate Rick, who sadly died this year (1996).

Acknowledgements

To all those lads and ladies who man the doors of Great Britain — I admire your bottle, especially to those that have died, paying the ultimate price, in the line of duty.

Thanks to Wayne Lakin, a good friend and a great Judoka for teaching me Judo and giving me a Coli.

To Kris Whelan for kindness and Greco Roman Wrestling.

To Alan Pethabrige, the Judo legend, for his kind help and friendship.

To Alan Peasland, my 24 hour training partner and friend — thanks Al.

To my friend Jamie O'Keef for his good advice and support.

To Alan Bardsley for making me 'dig deep', thank you sir.

To Paul Hobday for being a good friend.

To my first instructor in the 'way', still a legend, Mick Jackson.

Thanks to Sean McCarthy for the 'Lawrence of Arabia' quote.

To Maxine, a beautiful young lady - fond memories from Buster's night club.

Also as always - to my beautiful wife, Sharon.

God and the Bouncer all men adore
In times of trouble but not before
When the enemy's gone and the wrong is righted
God is forgotten — and the bouncer slighted.

Contents

Preface

Six men stood menacingly at the entrance to Buster's nightclub. It was 12.30 am on a busy Saturday night/Sunday morning. Muffled music, intertwined with the melée of a thousand voices, drifted out from the dance floor on a cloud of dry ice and tobacco smoke. There was a distinct smell of violence in the air that was as familiar to us as the smell of sizzling steak in a restaurant. The six, all uniform in their belligerence and bad attitude, had just been refused entry because three of them were wearing training shoes — against the dress code at this club — and the other three were too ugly and might have scared the other customers. Colin had told them so and they were not HP.

Some people take good advice and wander off to find a night spot that better suits their apparel. Others, like these, were not about to take 'no' for an answer. They were arguing the toss with Colin who was not the world's greatest conversationalist beyond 'you can't come in in trainers, you scruffy bastards!' so their case was falling on deaf ears.

I have to say that arguing with Colin was not an inspired idea when you consider that John 'Awesome' Anderson, sometimes known as 'one man gang' (because that's what he was) was ominously shadowing him looking not unlike a heavy from a sixties gangster movie. He had the kind of look that turned most men from 'hard to lard'. Both John and Colin were built like they don't build 'em any more. Their demeanour alone was usually enough to frighten the shit out of most would-be antagonists, but these birds had drunk a hole in the town and then pissed their faculties down the urinal at their last port of call.

John drew slowly and heavily on his cigarette, then blew the smoke provocatively into the face of the man with the mouth. The smoke hung momentarily in the summer night air as though taunting and then dissipated slowly. He casually flicked the butt. It spun in the air, almost in slow motion, spinning this way and that until it landed at the feet of the same man. He looked vexed but did not return the subliminal challenge.

John smiled — second time this year.

A volume was spoken in these two seemingly unfurnished gestures. The smoke, blown in the face, was a subliminal challenge that said 'Wanna dance?' and the flick of the butt was a reiteration of the challenge which said 'well, do ya?'. John was Clint Eastwood in black. He was ice cool and, though I don't smoke, this one action always impressed me the most. Wars had been won and lost with this latent discourse and yet it was still largely unknown outside of the arena where ambiguous parlance was the obligatory prerequisite to winning, or at least surviving a conflict.

It was only later, much later, when I had lived with violence and dipped my toe into the water that I understood his game:- Drawing back heavily on the cigarette was, to John, part of the 'duck syndrome', a way of hiding adrenal reaction and disguising fear. When the adrenalin flows one has an innate urge to take a sharp intake of breath, this inhalation feeds the working muscles with oxygen ready for fight or flight and also slows the flow of this natural bodily turbo drive — that many mistake for fear — until utilisation.

If un-disguised, the sharp gulp of air allows your opponent to see through you like a pane of glass, it tells him what you've got, who you are and what artillery — if any — you are holding. It also discloses a dossier on your experience in the arena and presents to him your 'armour chinks' on a platter.

These will be manipulated and engineered until he can drive a fucking tank through them — not a good thing when faced by a team hungry for a fight. It's a hard game, the rules are unspoken and capricious, and a good fighter will allow you to see 'armour chinks' that aren't really there. He uses them like pawns in a game of chess to draw in an inexperienced player, and before you know it, *checkmate*, the game is over. This one simple action spoke volumes about the experience of this man-monster who had eclipsed more mortals than NASA and regularly tore up malevolents like tissue at a snot party.

Pre-fight, the three seconds before 'take off' are mastered only by those that have lived the arena and 'danced the dance'. John was Nureyev, the master of the dance, and he was about to blot out some minnows who though they were great whites. These lads were getting louder by the minute and edging closer and closer to the entrance of the club and the doorway to violence. This closing of distance was, we all knew, a precursor to attack. We were being given an innate countdown. The leader of the pack was the effigy of antipathy, everything about him said 'violence', but we knew violence and understood his ilk. The forthcoming negotiations, what we knew as the 'interview', were simply a formality with these birds. Some you can talk down, others you can scare off, but with these we knew it was going to be a fight.

'Why can't we fucking come in,' asked the leader, who was ugly enough to come second in a one man beauty contest. The tone was challenging. He glanced down at his Nike training shoes and then back to Colin. 'These trainers cost me more than a ton,' he said, as though it might have made a difference. It didn't, he had more chance of flying to the moon.

Colin looked at him as though to say 'ask me do I give a fuck?' and said, 'You could have bought a new pair for that.'

Colin casually looked down at the offending footwear, like he was negotiating a piece of shit on the floor so as not to stand in it. His upper lip curled in a derisory way that said to anyone watching 'I don't care if they cost you a grand, they don't cross this doorway'.

The bird with the mouth edged forward to push past Colin who instinctively slapped his face. This was Colin's way of saying 'the interview is over, step back again and I'll make your head into a canoe'. There was an instant, long silence, the kind that you always get just before it kicks off; it was like the OK Corale.

John smiled. It was a gesture that told Enid Blighton's 'stupid six' that the time to talk was over. It was also another subliminal 'challenge to fight' that was as clear to street people as if it had have been sprayed on the wall. Sometimes in this arena there was no need for words, it was all done with gestures and ambiguous speak, and John was the master. The challenge was backed by a cool stare that made me feel glad to be on the right side of it.

He was my mentor and I studied him closely. When I looked at him I didn't see a meticulously smart half-caste man with a Gable moustache who spoke rarely and even then very quietly; I saw a whole university of empirical knowledge that seemed as deep as it was profound, I also saw the most effective fighting machine on two feet that you would ever wish to encounter. I was lucky enough to count him as my most personal tutor for a very busy five years.

After what had seemed like a lifetime, the slapped one felt his face, like they do in cheap Gung Fu movies.

'Is that your best shot?' he smiled, aggressively moving towards Colin once again. 'My sister can hit harder than that!'

'BANG!' John let him have it with a left hook that really oughta' be licensed with the police. He hit the deck with a sickly thud — he was out there with Pluto. John's face remained expressionless, as it always did. The other five would-be's moved back in a universal, yet silent, acceptance of defeat. Colin looked at John, a very small smile hit the right corner of his mouth, he then looked down at the unconscious man on the floor.

'Can she hit harder than that?' he asked.

Foreword

This is the third — possibly the last — of my bouncer series. The only reason it has reached the book shelves, and your eyes, is because people were gracious enough to buy *Watch My Back* & *Bouncer*, and I'd just like to thank those people very much. In this book I am regressing a little to the first night club I ever worked, a wonderful little place in Coventry called Buster's. For those who read *Watch My Back*, that was, basically, all based in Buster's night club.

I would like to introduce you to, and hopefully bring to life, some of the wonderful, colourful, brave, funny and often tragic people from that unique culture dish. Not just the doormen but also the other staff; from the glass collector who dreamed of being a doorman, to the receptionist who dreamed of falling in love with one of the doormen — any one of them would have done — and of being a model (model aircraft maybe!). The DJ (slippery deck) who fell in love with me — I didn't even know he was gay — and even a taxi driver, 'the Archbucket of Cuntabury' as 'Radio Rental' called him, who dreamed of having sex with one of the bar girls — any one of them would have done, also.

In *Watch My Back* I wrote predominantly about violence because at that time I was a violent hair trigger of a man who would fight at the drop of a hat — that's really what my environment and the times demanded — in *Bouncer*, though violence and violent people were still the main theme, I wrote more about philosophy and personal transition (sorry about that, I was going through a philosophical period), so it was more of a retrospective book. I'd just about finished working the doors at the time and was looking at it very much from a post-door perspective. It was a hard book to write because in recalling some of the horrific and violent incidents of my life on the door I sometimes couldn't believe that it was actually me that I was writing about and that I had knocked out all of those people and done those terrible things to other human beings — even though the bastards deserved every smack they took.

In *On The Door* I would like to write, again retrospectively, about the characters that influenced and guided me to where I am today (still in fucking Coventry!) and share with you some of the brilliant, happy, euphoric, crazy, sad, erotic, erratic and ecstatic moments of four years, in Buster's, at a time — the 80's — that is lost forever, except on the annals of my own mind. As with all the bouncer books I do tend to go off on a tangent and the stories very much tell themselves. They are not written in the order that they happened rather the order in which they are remembered. Much of this book is about Buster's, but I have also told of other places and other times.

Some of my stories I cannot tell because telling would mean hurting people that I love, and also because the facts might get me locked up. Sorry about that.

I hope you, whoever you are, enjoy what I have written. It goes without saying that all the stories are true, I wouldn't — and don't need to — make anything up just to sell a book. Some people have said that the fights I have written about are not true, which I find rather amusing, or that they have been exaggerated. A guy in the gym approached Awesome Anderson, and said,

'These stories in Geoff Thompson's books, are they exaggerated or made up?'

John said,

'To be completely honest there is a lot that he hasn't said, and in a few of the stories he has toned it down a little because of the legal angle.' Some things are better left un-said.

One of my friends, Ellis, a Coventry lad who knows me well rang me and said, laughing,

'Did you know, Geoff, that you weren't in half the fights that you said you were in Watch My Back?'

Then I started laughing.

'Is that right?'

'Yea,' he continued. 'I just had some young nob in the pub tell me all about it. Apparently he says it's true 'cus his mate told him and he comes from Coventry.'

'Well in that case,' I said, 'it must be right.'

Read the stories and make up your own mind, I don't really mind what people think: I know what's true and that's all that matters.

A bit of soap boxing: for the record, my views on life and violence have not changed. I stand by and still advocate all the philosophies I perused upon in my previous books about the door, which I have to say saddens me a little because I don't like violence, though I prefer to give it than to take it.

A few people were offended by what I had to say on the subject of violence and society and to those social hermits out there, to whom I am a barbarian with flawed character — an opinion to which they are entitled in a democratic society — remember this: when you fire your missiles of condemnation from a safe house some where in middle class suburbia, it is myself and the likes that shield and protect you and your fledglings from society's violent minority whilst you visit a night spot for your entertainment.

Whilst I'm not looking for a pat on the back I don't think I deserve a metaphoric boot in the bollocks either. For the record, my first response when confronted with a potentially violent situation is, when possible, avoidance. On the door this is usually an impossibility because you are paid to anticipate, interject and control violence and violent people.

My second response is escape; again this does not work when you are being paid to 'stay'. My third response is firm verbal dissuasion, something I learned and mastered in my time as a doorman, and my last response is to use physical force — before my antagonist has the chance to hit me — with a blow that will take him clean off the planet. I'll hit him so hard that when he wakes up his clothes will be out of fashion. I'll hit him so many times that he'll think he's surrounded. I'll be so deceptive that he won't know what, let alone who, and I'll hit him so accurately that he'll think he's in the twilight zone.

Often when facing a potential menace you learn, through experience, that avoidance, escape and dissuasion are not going to work and it is obvious to all but the blind that an attack is imminent so you by-pass responses 1-3 and go straight to response 4, physical. This is not gratuitous as some have said, it is survival, and though, from the outside looking in, it may seem a little overzealous it is not, it's a fucking absolute necessity. The body language and speak of a potential attacker tells the experienced exactly when, and if, he is going to be attacked: he almost gives you a countdown. Experience allows you to read this and pre-empt it. But, because the police and the law lords do not understand this attack ritual they do not support you when you are stood in the dock facing charges of assault and you end up in prison for your perception and their lack thereof.

It's very popular at the moment to make chic comments like 'violence is not the answer'. It has been said so often lately by the uninitiated that it has almost become a 'fucking' fashion accessory. Oh yea! Tell that to Andrew, one of the sweetest guys on the planet who has a lovely wife but struggles a little with bad nerves and keeps getting picked on by thugs because he is a 'soft touch'. I, and my ilk, allow Andrew to live a braver life by teaching him to fight back physically, and whilst he abhors violence and confrontation he dislikes it less than he and his lovely wife constantly being attacked.

I tell Andrew, as I tell everyone else who asks, that, metaphorically, self defence is a holstered gun hidden beneath a heavy overcoat only to be drawn when menace rears its ugly head. When you know how to use that metaphoric pistol, and your antagonists innately know that you know how to use it, sometimes you can beat them by just showing them the gun. You don't always have to pull the trigger.

Without counter violence how else are you going to stop the three men in front of you from stealing away your life and gang raping your wife, your daughter, or even your son? Wake up and smell the roses! Everybody knows that violence is not the long term solution — we are still searching for that holy grail like a blind man in a dark room searching for black pin that isn't there — but it surely is the short term answer, something to keep the rats at bay until the piper is called. The medical fraternity would call it 'toxin-anti toxin', poison against poison. Radiotherapy is not pleasant but it kills cancer. The long term solution is not the responsibility of the individual — that is a social problem — our responsibility is to protect our own until the bigger issue can be addressed.

Bailing water out of a sinking canoe may not address the root cause of your problem — the hole in the boat — but it's your only chance of getting to shore safely until it can be addressed. To all the do-gooders out there, let me tell you that pacifism is a luxury only enjoyed by those who have nothing or no one to protect, or whose belief in pacifism is stronger than that of love or need.

If you believe that you would not stick a glass into another human being's face, or bite him or butt him, answer me this question: unsolicited attackers are beating the shit out of you, and when they've finished they're going to rape your wife-son-daughter-mother-grandmother. You have one chance to stop this heinous crime, you can bite or stab or badly injure your assailant. What are you going to do? Well! What are you going to do?

This is not a hypothetical question, these crimes happen every day of the week, in every city, in every town. What are you going to do? Are you going to refuse to drop to such a level, and allow your loved one to be debased instead? I don't think so. So do me a favour and WAKE UP! Violence is off the reservation — someone has left the zoo unlocked and all the animals have escaped, only they're dressed in people suits. You have the opportunity, the unique opportunity, to prepare for battle, as Sun Tzu said, from a hundred miles away. Please don't stick your head in the sand and pretend that it is not happening — society is producing some absolute monsters who are enacting heinous crimes against innocents, and these cannot be overlooked. So, now that I have given my lecture, try not to look at myself and other doormen as bullying, violence-loving, power hungry Gorillas with a lust for blood; we are there to protect nice people from the types that have no morals and no feelings for your welfare. You are, to them, a meal ticket, nothing more — it's that simple. If you cannot comprehend that at this moment in time then, let me tell you, you will the very first time you encounter this human animal. As Ed Howe said, 'a good shock is often better than good advice'.

1. It's a Knock-out

'What's the problem lads?' My question was direct and hard.

'She won't fucking give us our coats, I've pointed them out to her. They're there, look, there.'

He pointed at two jackets in the middle of a hundred more hanging from coat racks in the tiny cloakroom in the tight reception area of Buster's night club. I looked at the girl. Blonde, pretty and thicker than a whale omelette.

'They haven't got a ticket, Geoff.' Her voice was scared and I gave her a wink to let her know that I would deal with it. That was my game, what I was paid to do. I felt the ever-so familiar tingle of adrenalin as it got in place for fight or flight, only in this game there was no flight, you either stayed or you didn't work. 'Runners' got black-balled from every club in the city the very first time they listened to natural instinct and broke the minute mile. 'Bottling it' also crushed hard earned kudos and self belief flatter than an indent, it did for your confidence and reputation what leprosy does for your social life. They say that you are only as good as your last fight and it's true, you could be the bravest man on earth for a hundred fights and become a 'door outcast' by bottling it once. Not fair, methinks, but that, as Esther might say, is life.

This particular night had been a little slow. I'd just come back from the toilet, where the big nobs hang out, to find these two guys arguing with the cloakroom girl. I have to say that she was a nice little thing, though a bit thick, and thought fellatio was an Italian opera, you know the type. The guys arguing with her were in their mid-twenties, scruffy looking, hard eyed men with barbed attitudes and scowling faces. The story was that both had lost their cloakroom tickets and could not prove that they had placed jackets in the care of the club.

Of course they wanted to claim their jackets all the same. The girl had explained that they had to wait until the end of the night for their jackets if they could not produce a ticket. That's the club rules, it was nothing personal. They said she was 'fucking useless' and insisted that she 'give us our jackets if you know what's good for you'.

I splayed my arms in front, blocking the gap between me and the two men. This was my 'fence'. Verbal dissuasion started,

'Lads, you know the crack. You need a ticket. No ticket no jacket.'

'Yea, I know but look,' he pointed at the jackets again, scruffy looking leathers that looked more like cleaning shammies, 'they're there.'

'So give me your tickets and you can take them.'

'She fucking told you didn't she. We've lost the tickets.' He raised his voice challengingly, and moved towards me as he spoke. He was testing me out. It had worked with the young girl, now he was trying it with me. This was almost a subliminal challenge which I met and surpassed, as he moved towards me and I stopped him with my lead hand fence. I was controlling the play. I picked up the aggression to meet the challenge. It was a game and I was used to playing it.

'Yea and she also told you that you don't get the fucking jackets with out the fucking tickets. All right!?' I deliberately included the expletive to raise the play and speak their speak. I stared both of them down as I said it. The bird with the mouth became submissive because my aggression had out-leagued him.

'Come on man, just let us have the jackets. They're ours, honestly.'

I'll be honest, I didn't like the guys — they were big mouthed bullies. If I hadn't arrived when I did they'd have already taken the jackets and hurt the girl if she'd stepped in the way, so I was in no mood to do them any favours.

'No. You'll have to either wait till the end of the night or leave the club and come back for them later.'

They looked at each other hesitantly. Should they go for it or not? They stormed out of the night club mumbling something about 'coming back'. The little girl in the cloakroom smiled, and thinking that I was her hero, I smiled back. To be honest I never really thought any more about the incident until about 2.30 in the morning when the guys returned. Everyone else had gone home bar me, John and Dave the manager of the club.

'What are these two after?' The manager asked, looking at the CCTV screen in the corner of his small, cluttered office. Two men were walking menacingly towards the doors of the club.

'Probably after their jackets, I wouldn't give 'em them earlier because they didn't have a ticket.'

John drew on his cigarette.

'They don't look too happy Geoff.' There was no emotion in his voice.

'Well,' I continued, 'they had a go at the cloakroom girl earlier and they weren't happy when I wouldn't give them their coats.'

The doors to the club banged violently. We watched the lads, on screen, as they kicked and punched the doors. They were unaware that we could see them. At the time the cameras were a secret known only to the club staff.

'Looks like they want some!' John commented.

'Yea, I think you're right,' I replied, still watching them on screen. A burst of adrenalin hit my belly and ran through my veins. I sniffed heavily, as though I had a cold, to hide the natural inhalation that comes with fight or flight. My legs began their pre-fight shake. I tapped my foot to the sound of an imaginary beat to hide it.

'Well they've certainly come to the right place,' added the manager with a grin. He was our biggest fan. We liked him too. He had stuck with us through thick and thin over the years and had lied to the police, on our account, enough times to warrant an honours degree in perjury.

John and I walked out of the office to the entrance doors. A violent encounter awaited us. It felt no different than going into a sparring session with your mates at the gym, but that was only because our training sessions were more brutal than the real thing — well, we wanted to get it right, no sense in taking the word of some ancient whose last fight, honourable as it might have been, was against a Samurai on horse back. The enemy had changed; the environment had changed also, so logically the 'arts' had to change too. Only, when you try and tell many of today's traditionalists this they don't hear you because they've got their sycophantic heads stuck up the arse of some eastern master.

John opened the front doors of the club, the sound of the metal locks echoing into an empty night. He stood in the doorway, taking it all up, and stared at the two men. That should have been enough, they should have read the 'don't fuck' sign emblazoned across his face like a Christmas banner but they were blind to what was patently obvious to us: they were way, way out of their league.

'Wot d' ya want?' John was blunt. He frit the shit out of me and he was on my side.

The smaller one got straight to the point. He'd had a long night, he was pissed at me and the club and the whole fucking world by the looks of him and he told us so. He obviously hadn't done his homework on 'street speak' and didn't know that he was already in quicksand up to his scrawny little neck otherwise he would have shut his big mouth and broken the minute mile — in the opposite direction.

Someone once said to me,

'What do you reckon you could do against a man like John Anderson, Geoff?'

'Oh about sixty mile an hour!' I replied.

'We've come for our fucking jackets,' said number one.

'Yea,' number two echoed like a parrot, 'you're fucking out of order not giving them to us earlier.'

I popped my head out of the door over John's shoulder. As soon as they saw me they lit up like luminous nodders, which was appropriate because they were both 'nobs'.

'Yea, he's the one, he's the wanker that wouldn't give us them earlier on. Out of order.' He stabbed the air aggressively with his finger to underline 'out of order'.

Wanker!? Me? I'm not sure that I deserved the title and I have to say it annoyed me somewhat.

'You didn't get the coats earlier on because you didn't have the tickets and if you don't watch your mouth you won't fucking get them now. All right?'

John grabbed the coats from the cloakroom and held them at arm's length out of the door. As the lads went to take them off him, sure that they had already won because they were getting what they'd come for, he dropped them on the floor at their feet. Grudgingly, amidst a few inaudible mumbles they picked the coats up and dusted them down, a bit like polishing a turd. As they walked away, slipping their arms into the leathers, number one said, hammering the nails into his own coffin,

'We'll be back for you two. You've got a big problem.'

As one John and myself stepped out of the door towards them.

'Don't bother coming back, do it now?' I challenged.

'Yea! Yea! Why not? Lets do it!' number one said, accepting the challenge. His chest heaved and his arms splayed, his speak became fast and erratic — I knew that he was ready to 'go'. Number two's face dropped in disbelief, his chin nearly hit the floor. He looked at his mate as though to say 'shouldn't we have talked about this?' He was obviously in no hurry to get his face punched in and had a lot more intelligence. He put on his best pleading look, raised his arms submissively and retreated away from us quicker than a video rewind.

It was nearly 3 am, pitch black but for the fluorescent lights at the entrance of the club that lit our arena. The air was thick with quiet, less the galloping hearts and frightened bowel movement of our opponents. The manager stood at the doorway like a pugilistic time keeper about to witness the mis-match of the century. He shook his head knowingly as John and I squared up for the match fight with the two unhappy campers. He had seen John and myself in action more times than he cared to remember and felt sorry for the lads in front of us, one of whom foolishly thought he was in with a fighting chance. He had more chance of getting an elephant through a cat flap.

I must admit though that he did have me a little worried — I was scared I might kill him.

John raised his guard like a boxer, mine was at half mast like a karataka. My man raised his own guard high and ready, covering his face in an amateurish boxing guard, heavily exposing his midriff. His stance was short and off balance. His ribs looked mighty suspect.

Adrenal deafness clicked in and tunnel vision locked onto my opponent as he moved in a semi circle, to my left and around me. These were reactions to the adrenal syndrome. Blood is pumped to all the areas in the body that are seen as vital in fight or flight, like the major muscle groups. The extra blood needed is drawn away from those areas that are seen as non vital, like certain sections of the brain and the internal organs — this is why we experience time distortion, time loss, memory distortion and memory loss in post-fight. The adrenalin also acts as anaesthesia during confrontation so even the pain of broken bones may be overcome for long enough to survive.

John's opponent took one look at him and lost the fight in Birmingham. He said,

'You're a boxer aren't you. Fuck that. I don't want to fight you.'

He was wrong. John wasn't a boxer — though he could box a bit — he was far worse. I started to move in for the kill.

From my experience many people lose the fight before it even begins, in Birmingham as I'm fond of saying, because they mistake the natural feelings associated with combat for sheer terror and allow their inner opponent the run of their head. I remember the story of a wonderful old wrestler from London called Bert Asarati. Unfortunately he is dead now and that is our loss, but in his day he was a monster of a wrestler with a fearsome reputation for hurting his opponents, even when it was a show match. He was seventeen stone at only five foot six and a fearsome fighter. He was so big that when he sat on a train or a bus he took up two seats — a fearsome man whose reputation preceded him.

Another wrestler of repute was travelling down by train from Glasgow to fight Mr Asarati in a London arena. All the way down on the train journey the Glaswegian ring fighter kept thinking about the arduous task that lay ahead, and every time the train stopped at a station his inner opponent would tempt him to get off the train and go back to Glasgow. Every time he thought about the forthcoming battle with Mr Asarati his adrenalin went into overdrive. He was more scared than he could ever remember being. His un-captained fear was starting to cause massive self doubt and he began to wonder whether he was even fit to be in the same ring as the great man. Every time the train stopped at a station the self doubt grew, propagated by his inner opponent who constantly reminded him of the prowess of Mr Asarati, and of how Mr Asarati was going to 'hurt him' when they got in the ring. At every station the inner opponent got louder and stronger, the adrenalin grew stronger also and the wrestler's bottle gradually slipped more and more out of his grasp until, in the end, he could take no more. At Birmingham station he got off and caught the next available train back to Glasgow. He sent a note to Bert Asarati which read, 'Gone back to Glasgow, you beat me in Birmingham.' His inner opponent had beaten him a hundred miles before he even got to the fight venue.

This is what often happens to people in street situations. This is what happened to John's opponent on this night. He didn't lose the fight to John; he lost it to himself. John, not one to hit a man that didn't want to fight, moved away and let his prey go.

I buried a low round house kick, as an opener to see what my opponent had got, into his ribs. As I had surmised they were indeed suspect. He doubled over in pain and I swept his feet from under him. He lay on the floor like an upturned turtle. I didn't have the heart to go in for the finish, he was no match at all so I let him back up again and played for a while shooting kicks to his head — something I would not have tried had the man been any threat at all — and continually sweeping him to the floor without hurting him too much. Every time he got back up I swept him back down.

In the end I felt sorry for him and told him to 'fuck off home' before I really did hurt him. He got angry at this and ran at me with arms flailing so I dropped him with a low side kick in the belly and followed with a heavy punch to his jaw.

BANG!

He hit the deck heavily and I heard the familiar sickly crack of bone on pavement. He lay before me like an unconscious thing. I wondered whether he was badly hurt. For a second he looked all right then, to my horror, a huge pool of blood appeared like a purple lake around his head. I thought I'd killed him. The pool got bigger and darker by the second. His face was death-like, pale and debauched.

He still didn't wake up.

I felt panic in the pit of my stomach like a bowling ball. My life passed before me. John walked over and looked down at the blooded heap.

'Good punch Geoff,' he said as though I'd just performed a nice technique on the bag in the gym.

I felt terrible. He looked dead and the blood intimated that perhaps I had cracked his skull. I waited for the brains to seep through with the blood then realised that the guy probably didn't have any to lose. His mate looked on, shaking his head as though thinking 'I knew this was going to happen'.

'Is he dead?' he asked, adding to my misery. At the word 'dead' my stomach exploded.

WHOOSH!! The adrenalin of aftermath shot through me like a fast thing and I couldn't stay there any longer. I wandered back into the club to grab a drink and calm myself down. This was my first KO on the door — I didn't even know how I had done it — and it scared the shit out of me. At the bar I shook like a leaf and made a promise to God that I would never hit any one again if only he would let this one live, a promise I made every time I KO'd some unfortunate with an eye for my title, and broke every time they recovered.

Erasmus said that (no, he didn't work at Buster's) 'war is delightful to those who have had no experience of it'. He was right, fighting doesn't look so nice when you view it from this angle. Outside John lifted the unconscious man's head out of the blood bath with his foot to see the extent of the damage. Blood was still issuing from his head and making an explosion transfer right across the whole of one paving slab.

'Is he dead?' his mate asked again, almost as though he wanted him to be, something to talk about on a Sunday afternoon in the pub.

John gave him one of those looks and he shut his mouth. Inside the club, already contemplating the 'big house' and life in a cell with a right forearm like fucking Popeye — or a very close cell mate — I made my way to the manager's office and watched the fight on the CCTV recording, just to see how bad I would look should the police get their hands on a copy of the tape. My hands shook with trepidation as I pressed 'Play' and watched as the scenario silently re-ran on the small screen. It looked bad though it lacked the sounds and smells of what had just occurred. Somehow being on screen had lost the debacle its ugliness.

I'm ashamed to say that I almost admired the action as I watched myself battering this non-entity, even using the 'slow mo' to highlight the meaty parts and check out my fighting technique. Sadly I, like most, had become desensitised to 'screen scraps' from a lifetime of watching 'empty' vignettes of violence crafted by screen technicians to stir inspiration via simulated battles.

Someone once said that if they could put smell into cinema every war film ever made would flop at the box office. They were right. What the recorder held, and showed, of a fight that had frightened the shit out of me did little more in replay than make me smile at how easy it had looked. It makes me smile when I see how great producers creatively weave the sow's ear of real violence into the silk purse of celluloid. It would seem that the hypocrisy of people knows no bounds. Millions, who abhor brutality, flock to view 'justified' killings and glorious Oscar winning deaths, enacted by handsome thespians with carved features and rehearsed pros. The wowed, entranced audience visualising their finger on the killing trigger and their own wives behind the mourner's veil at a hero's funeral.

I was sickened, and at once enlightened, by what I had felt. I quickly re-wound the video and scrubbed the fight off the tape, then rewound it again and gave it a second scrub, just to be sure. In court tackle like that could hang a fella. Back up to the bar in the empty club, I helped myself to another drink.

I felt sick with worry. I felt confused by the feelings that ran through my body. At once I was scared by what I had done and yet, in part, I felt exhilarated by the fact that I had knocked a fellow unconscious. I was ashamed of myself, but that's how I felt. It was probably partly due to the fact that, after adversity, the body releases endorphines, a natural morphine, into the blood. These give you a 'pick up' and make you feel high, I guess that's where the confusion begins. Happy and sad at the very same moment, what a paradox. Years later, after many more KO's and sleepless nights and talks with God, I would develop a tighter control over this panic and learn better to live with fear. For now I had to contend with the ignorance that came with being a 'greenhorn'.

Back outside my unconscious opponent finally came around. Blood lay like a pillow around his head and hung to his hair and face like goo as he lifted his head from the pavement.

His hair was matted in the stuff; he looked like he'd been machine gunned.

His mate stared as though he had seen a ghost, as he rose from the dead.

'We thought you were a gonna.' He smiled as he said it.

John shot him another angry glance.

'Sorry,' the bird mumbled, then, 'well I did.'

John looked at the floor at the three broken teeth laying forlorn on the concrete. He thought they looked a little bizarre without the attachment of gums. When the guy had been KO'd he'd obviously landed on his face and smashed out his teeth. He followed John's glance to the floor and his eyes squinted as though struggling to focus on the fact that he was looking at his own teeth. It was the first time he had ever seen them out of a mirror or a photo. He quickly felt his mouth and the numb, blooded and gnarled gap where the same teeth used to reside.

'Your mate's knocked some of my teeth out,' he complained to John, stating the obvious.

'There's no hiding anything from you, is there? If you don't fuck off quick I'll knock the rest of them out.'

John found me at the bar looking pale and very worried. I was still thinking about prison and wondering whether this job was really for me. I didn't like the feeling of losing my liberty to a wanker like the one outside collecting his teeth for the tooth fairy. The picture of unconsciousness and a blood splattered pavement stuck in my head like a freeze frame. In that moment of wonderment Napoleon Bonaparte came to mind — doesn't Napoleon always fucking do that to ya — when he said (not to me personally of course, the man's been dead for ages) that there is nothing like the sight of a battle field after the fight to inspire princes with a love of peace and a horror of war. I had just seen the battle field and felt that inspiration. Unfortunately I was to experience it a lot more, and far worse than this before I learned the lesson and dumped 'the door' in a transitional leap for a better, less violent existence.

John broke my daydream and ended my agony.

'Don't worry, he's all right, you just knocked his teeth out. Nothing bad.'

A sigh of relief raced through my body like a death row reprieve.

'Thank fuck for that!' I was thanking fuck when I should have been thanking God, sadly I'm ashamed to say, he had already been forgotten in the elation.

'Don't get too complacent, though, Geoff. He's a wanker, he'll go to the police. I know the type.'

'That's OK,' I thought. 'I can live with that. As long as he isn't 'brown bread'.'

We were pretty sure that the police would get involved because it was a wounding. Broken bones and blood meant a probable charge of Section 18 with intent which carried a possible five years in prison. So, as always, we, me John and Dave got out stories sorted out ready, just in case. The video had already been doctored, twice, so that wasn't a problem. Dave agreed to say that he had switched the video off at 02.30am. John and I agreed to say that the men did turn up at 02.45am and that we gave them their coats and sent them on their jolly way. A bit belligerent but unhurt.

John was right. Within two days of the incident we'd had a visit from plod and were both taken in for a statement. As planned we recited to our stories like lines from a bad play. 'No. I didn't hit the man, officer. That would be breaking the law. Must have fell down the stairs' — that sort of scenario. And why not, the police are always covering themselves with 'accidents and stairs', even when they happen to reside in a station that has no stairs.

'He fell down the stairs M' Lord!'

'What, ten times, officer?'

This is one of the things we always did at Buster's, and did it well, whenever there was a altercation that we thought might attract attention from plod we would immediately work out our story so that, if/when arrested, there was no confusion or contradiction. Our aim was, hopefully, to get the charges thrown out at 'station level', if not next best was to get it thrown out by the CPS (Crown Prosecution Service). If the evidence was 50-50 — they said we hit them, we said we didn't — the CPS had a rep for not proceeding with charges because it would be a waste of taxpayers' money dragging a case through the courts when there was little chance of a conviction or prosecution. Why waste it on us when they could waste it on so many other things. If the police couldn't make a decision at station level they would automatically refer the case to the CPS. In turn, if they thought they might not get a conviction, they too would throw the case out and all charges would be dropped like the proverbial 'hot brick'. It was a system that always worked well for us — touch wood.

Unfortunately it is nigh on impossible to work the door within the law, unless of course you are a high ranking police officer who says, and believes, that you should 'never hit first, it's not necessary' or some fucking silly psychiatrist type woman, who looks as though she put her make-up on in a street fight, that gives you the 'never make bodily contact with a person, it sends out all the wrong signals' scenario. Oh yea, so how do we stop the monster with a face like ten boxers from coming into the club when he's barred, or get him out if he is playing up? Just ask him politely and hope that he goes? Or keep asking him until he goes? Be firm but fair?

'Now listen to me me fella me lad if you don't jolly well leave the club right this instant — or as soon as you're ready — I'm going to have to..to..ask you to leave again, only next time I'll be jolly well firmer than this!'

It might work in cartoon land where exploded cats get up, unhurt and live to chase the mice another day. In the real world? I don't think so. What planet are these people on? A planet called hypothesis, methinks, where everything works in life just like it does in theory, a place where there is no violence and mankind lives on love. There is a place like this where these concepts might work, it's called the moon, and it only works there because it's pretty fucking uninhabited. Don't these people just kill you? I'd have more time for them if they did the job for a year, and tried to work their concepts with 'real people'. Believe me it wouldn't happen, I guarantee it: within two weeks the police commissioner chappy would be nutting everything that moved and the physiologist would be only employing behaviourism to make windows for the perfunctory 'hand bag strike to the temple' of the guy who is going to rape her senseless unless she gets fucking violent fucking quick.

So, sometimes, on the door we would have to tailor our stories so that they fitted a law that was unkind to those whose job it was to stop others breaking it.

'John, my good man, the story is a little fat and won't fit into this blasted law thing. What I propose we do, me fella is slim the blighter down with a diet of half truths so that it does fit!'

It's interesting that a man called Ghengis Khan, thought of by many as a barbarian, said that the British were uncivilised because the law of the land did not protect the people. We made it protect us by lying; it was either that or become a victim of its often archaic precept.

We always kept the story simple leaving very little to remember. We never allowed the police, the little devils, to draw anything from us that we didn't want to say. They play the game very deviously, as John and I were about to find out. As luck would have it 'broken teeth' was hated by plod because he had 'previous' for police assault. They don't like villains who attack their own and had no intention of helping him too much. In the old days the fella would definitely have been exposed to the 'accident with stairs' scenario that was almost the perfunctory penalty for 'beating copper', but with things the way they are now that is no longer a feasible option if an officer values his pension and wants to remain in employment.

Things have changed, I think for the worse, and anyone with a grudge can attack a policeman without fear of reprisal. He'll probably walk away with little more than a metaphoric slap on the wrist. The police might as well change their uniforms and wear targets on their chest and helmet. Robin Williams says that in New York a policeman will shout to a robber,

'Stop or I'll blow your fucking head off!'

In Britain a bobby is more likely to shout,

'Stop . . . or I'll be forced to shout STOP again!'

Of course, taking power away from policemen did curtail police injustice and hamper the minority officers who abused their powers — he was only ever in the minority and could have been controlled 'in house' — but it also took away the majority's protective fence that stopped the villains in society from abusing our officers. Thankfully this disease has not yet spread to the door — though it won't be long I think — you hit a doorman and, if the team is worth its salt, you'll pay in blood. That's the unwritten law.

In the interview room the atmosphere was tense and I practised the 'duck syndrome' to hide the fact that I was experiencing adrenalin. If she, the plain clothes DC interviewing me, could see my fear she might rightly assume that I was lying through my teeth. I was, of course, I had become a master of the lie, but, I thought rather un-Christianly, at least they were not broken teeth. Let the games begin!

'This guy was a bit of a wanker, wasn't he, Geoff?' WDC was trying to get into my confidence. I wished she was trying to get into my pants — she was gorgeous.

'Absolutely.' I knew the game, I'd played it with better players too, though none so delicious as this one.

'That's why you gave him some pain?'

'Pain? I don't remember giving him any of that.' I was so convincing that even I was starting to believe that I was innocent.

'I told you already Jane,' (that was her name, we were on first name terms but only because she wanted to hang me), 'I didn't touch him. I had no reason too. He was just a mouthy youth with a fetish for abuse. Nothing more. Probably got dropped by someone less tolerant than me on his way home.'

'Yea I know you said that, Geoff, but we both know that you did it. And I don't blame you. He's a pleb, a lemon. Deserved all the pain that you gave him. Off the record Geoff, why did you hit him?'

Ah, the old 'off the record' hook, the old 'we don't blame you' trick, the 'let's pretend that we're on his side and then fuck him senseless' ploy. It'll be flattery next, mark my words. I wondered if I might get a cup of coffee and a date out of this?

'Any chance of a cup of coffee Jane?'

Worth a try.

'Yea, sure. I'll just fetch one. White with sugar?'

'Yea. Thanks.'

Yippee! One down — one to go. The coffee was machine made but welcome. Actually it could have been soup, you can never tell, can you? I thanked her effusively.

'So. You were going to tell me why you hit him.'

I was?!

'I just told you, Jane, I didn't hit him.' I was going to tell her that he looked better without teeth anyway but thought better of it.

'You're a bit of a Karate man, aren't you Geoff? Was it a Karate kick that you hit him with?'

Yawn — now the flattery ploy — I wonder when she's going to get into a world of 'your mates told us everything' to get me to own up. I tried not to smile but I couldn't help myself and a small grin cracked on my lips. I felt a belly chuckle rousing down below but held onto it for dear life. This was a serious business.

'I never laid a glove on the guy.'

'Geoff, we know what happened, your mate's already told us. This is off the record. I'm just interested in what happened out there.'

Jane was a beautiful women, a cracker. I fell in love instantly. She was tall, curvaceous with dark brown hair and a figure to die for. I liked her a lot. She looked tough in a womanly kind of way and I couldn't help examining the curves so delicately pronounced through her dark blue skirt and white nylon blouse. There was a faint hint of nipple peeping through, it wasn't cold so I pretentiously surmised that it must have been me. I'd heard of this DC before and by all accounts she was a good girl with loads of bottle. Apparently she could 'have a fight' as well. I liked that in a woman.

As we sat in the tiny interview room at the police station Jane gently questioned me about my statement, trying to trick and trip me. I did my best to answer her as untruthfully as I could. That wasn't too hard. What was hard was stopping myself from staring. I love a woman in uniform.

John wasn't so lucky, all he got was a bold beat cop with a bad attitude and halitosis — his breath could kill a fly at five yards. His head shone like a polished apple and hair grew out of his nose in strands that looked like little spiders legs sticking out of his nostrils. It looked as though his head hair was growing inside out. He was the most un-attractive man in the world and he wreaked of antiquated, soap smelling after shave that he'd obviously washed with that morning. The paunch that hung over his belt looked like a shirt full of scrumped apples, his trousers were worn in 70's fashion — far too tight around the crutch and an inch short on the length. It looked as though the turn-ups had fallen out with his shoes. He tried to talk the talk with John but he was swapping speak with the wrong guy. John told him so.

'Listen. You're wasting your breath (bad breath at that) trying that old muck on me. I've heard it all before and from more convincing people than you. So don't waste you time.'

Damn, back to the drawing board.

As Jane walked me out of the station, after two hours of questioning, she gave it one last shot. It was her parting shot.

'Must have been a really good kick to do that much damage Geoff. What was it that started it all, anyway?'

I stopped and looked at this beautiful woman before me. I have to say that I was disappointed. She must have thought me thicker than shortbread to fall for this shit. She should have had a little more respect. I let her see that I was fed up with the silly games. She knew and I knew that if they had anything on me, I mean anything at all, we wouldn't have been talking in the hallway of the police station with me on the way out. We'd be conversing through the bars of a cell.

'What are you trying to say, Jane?' I said it in a kind of pissed off way.

For a second she was silent. She had sensed my disappointment.

'Nothing,' she said quietly, 'it doesn't matter.'

I made my way out of the station and home. I was not charged. When I told John that Jane had tried to trick me he laughed his nuts off. In a way everyone was happy, except 'broken teeth' who now talks with a whistle. The police were happy because a known police attacker had caught some karma and we were happy because we got away with it, once again. I did get to meet Jane later in a personal capacity: we laughed about the incident and became friends, she was a beautiful woman. Jane, if you are out there, 'Big Kisses'.

2. Sweet Dreams?!

Some nights when I worked the door I felt ill with tiredness. I was working five days a week on the building sites — at the time I was a hod carrier — 4-6 nights on the door, trying to train every day as well and fit in time with my wife and kids. At the weekends it wasn't so bad because the club got very busy and the time went very quickly, you hardly had a minute to think about sleep. But when you got the real quiet nights minutes often felt like hours and hours like days. Some nights, especially between Christmas and new year when everyone had spent up and over indulged, you might only get a handful of people turn up to the club, but you still had to be there. I remember one night when we had only two people in the whole club and somehow, I don't quite know how, they ended up fighting and we had to throw them out, leaving the club empty but for the staff. The manager went mad.

'Where's the two punters?' he asked.

'I had to throw them out, they were fighting!' I said, almost embarrassed.

'What the fuck did they find to fight about in an empty club?' asked the manager. I shrugged my shoulders. People will always find a reason to fight, even in an empty night club.

This particular night, I think it was a Wednesday, I was absolutely cream crackered, I was so tired that I felt like dying. Every time I sat down, even for a minute, the demon tiredness came over me like a trance. I had to jump up quick before I was in a deep sleep and away for the night.

One night I was so tired I even fell asleep leaning at the DJ consul, pretty fucking dangerous when you consider that the DJ was gay and fancied me. I could have woken up with an arsehole the size of Blackwall Tunnel. I sat down on the comfy armchair in the little cloakroom at the front door of the club; I had to rest my legs and just close my eyes for a second, I was so desperately tired. I was on 'till 2am and it was still only 12.30. An hour and a half to go.

John and Colin stood at the doorway of the cloakroom to cover me so that no one could see if I dropped off. I thought this was very good of them until I realised that they wanted me to fall asleep so that they could 'play'. I only wanted to close my eyes for a couple of minutes, I'd be all right then I felt sure. I closed my eyes and a deep sleep fell upon me. Before I knew it I had drifted off and was in sleepsville. The sounds of music and revellers fell to a distant hum and it was absolute bliss. I was so far gone that, to all intents and purposes, I might as well have been tucked up back home in my own bed. It felt great. My dreams though were far from the sweet variety and the next few minutes were to be troublesome, to say the least. In the far off distance I could hear the reverberation of conviviality, there was much giggling. Voices floated in and out of my consciousness like unwanted visitors and poked at my tranquillity. My sleep felt uncomfortable and claustrophobic. I could feel the crush of bodies all around me, their laughing indicated that they were obviously having a damn good time — but at whose expense?

'Just a dream Geoff,' I told myself, then, convinced, I fell into a deeper sleep.

Something brushed against my mouth. I twitched my nose, as you do, but continued sleeping. Probably the 'feather under the nose' scenario that your mates always enact when you steel a few ZZZZZ's. I wasn't in the mood, I just wanted to sleep. I re-adjusted my head to regain the comfortable position. Back to the coziness of my dreams. Bliss.

More giggling, more discomfort, men and women this time and a general feeling of uneasiness and crush. I adjusted my position yet again because something kept tickling my face and mouth. The vexation grew closer and the giggling louder. My dreams were becoming nightmares.

A frustrated voice in my head shouted, 'leave me alone I just wanna sleep!' There it was again, something tickling my lips, it was heavy and smelt musty — there was no way that was a fucking feather!

AHHHHHH!!!!!! I awoke with a start to find a big black willy dangling over my mouth: it was Colin's, he was straddled over me with his dick hanging just above my mouth and he was being gee'd on by John and a bunch of other people that had crowded into the small cloakroom. I let out a second involuntary scream and ran from the room. Oh the shame of it!

Colin tumbled to the floor gagging hysterically and John laughed till tears flowed as I shuffled moodily up the club to get ten glasses of coke to swill my mouth out just in case. It was frightening, the closest I ever came to being a 'cock sucker'.

Funnily enough this cured my drowsiness, my tiredness disappeared and I was wide awake. There was probably only a couple of hundred people in the club that night, most were around the bar area where I stood drinking my coke. It was an S-shaped bar that appeared to be cut out of a rock, in fact the whole club looked like an underground cavern. The glass collector approached me with a worried look on his face. I shook my head in disgust, still thinking about my near miss with fellatio, and I was sure the glass collector was going to make some smug remark about it to wind me up. He didn't, he looked concerned.

'See them two men at the corner over there, Geoff?' he pointed over to the nook of the bar, a little area set out for him to load and wash the glasses.

I nodded.

'They're givin' me grief. Every time I try to put my glasses on the bar they refuse to move and tell me to 'fuck off'.'

To be honest this was a common occurrence. Punters get a spot by the bar and they just don't want to move. All the glass collectors we had at Buster's were very young, easy targets for the bullying types that often frequent a rough night club like this one. I looked over at the lads. They were leaning against the bar and facing the dance floor like a pair of John Waynes.

'Leave it with me,' I said, gulping some more coke as visions of my 'close encounter' rushed into my head. An involuntary shuddered ran down my spine.

The glass collector had looked really scared and it made me hate the bullying bastards by the bar all the more. I was once like this young, impressionable lad, scared and bullied by people and feelings that I didn't understand. I approached the men to tell them to move. In reality I should have gotten one of the other doormen to watch my back but, at the time I was still smarting from the practical joke in the cloak room — it took me a while to live that one down — and anyway I didn't really think there was too much of threat.

'Excuse me lads, but you'll have to move from the bar, the glass collector needs this space to load his glasses. Sorry about that.'

The moment I spoke to these fucking lemons was the first moment that I hated them. I instinctively knew from that second that we'd be fighting. The arrogance just poured from them like shit from a sewer pipe. They looked at me, smirked, then looked at each other and smiled. They didn't reply to my request they just carried on scanning the dance floor as though I was fucking invisible. Both were about the same height and build as me — big, broad, good looking types. One wore a faded denim jacket turned up at the cuffs like a seventies cast off. A heavy gold bracelet hung on his tattooed right wrist like a heavy thing. His mate sported a Roman nose that seemed to go right into his forehead — it should have had a sign on it saying 'break me'. His upper lip was wide like a Lion and his teeth were straight and white, which was a pity because he was spending his last few minutes attached to them.

I later found out that these two plebs were big in their own arena and liked to throw their weight about. What they failed to realise was that this was our arena and we were not bullying amateurs, we were paid professionals, people who really could 'have a fight'. A lot of local bullies meet their karma when they step out of their own little ponds and get eaten up by bigger fish. Having said that, the door is not really about having a fight — although that is a part of it and an integral part — it is more about protecting people and property from those in society who do not wish to follow the peaceful way.

Most of these little wankers, like the two facing me now in this story, actually come out looking for trouble. To them a fight in, or after, the night club is as perfunctory as a mint after dinner; a weekend without a fight is a bad weekend. But they were not fighters, they were not hard men, most of them couldn't fight the tide in the bath, but they thought they could and that's exactly what made them dangerous. The bottom line is men like these two kill nice people in bar fights. My job as a doorman was firstly to understand these people — understand the enemy as Sun Tzu would say — to anticipate them, help them to avoid trouble, to escape a physical response by using verbal dissuasion, then, and only if all else had failed me, take them off the planet with a pre-emptive attack that stopped them quicker than a 50 MPH 3000lb Ford Cortina across the knees (believe me that stops them). Doing the door is about avoiding violent confrontation but equally it is about protecting yourself should you think the aggressor is going to turn nasty.

'You listening to me. Move away from the bar so that the lad can get his glasses in.' This time I upped the aggression and backed the verbal with a stare that challenged both to move or be moved.

'Yea, sure. We'll move. But what about those guys over there?'

It was a delaying tactic that annoyed me. Why don't people just do as you ask? It saves a lot of pain in the long term. He pointed to a couple of other lads further down the bar who were also in the way of the glass collector's hatch, but less so than they.

'Don't worry about them. That's my job. I'll deal with them.'

They still didn't move and partly I felt it might have been a little bravado, you know, not wanting to be seen to be moved on by the doormen. So I thought I'd do a bit of loopholing. I moved away for a second so that they could shift of their own accord and not have it look as though they'd lost face. I walked over to the other lads by the bar and asked them politely to move from the bar. Without any hesitation they did as I asked. I looked across to see the other two still standing arrogantly in the same place. Backs to the bar, leaning on their elbows with their chests sticking out in front like pigeons: the pomposity was almost palpable. I felt the adrenalin rise as I walked over once again, I also felt anger. These lads had been given plenty of chances, and they were about to be given one more — their last.

'I have asked you three times now to move from here and . . .'

'Yea, yea, yea! Fuck me, you said already. We'll move when we're ready.' They cut me dead, mid sentence, and my anger rose dramatically. I could feel a right cross loading up, itching at my hip. As they spoke they didn't even have the respect to look at me. They had obviously read me wrong. They would pay for that miscalculation, everyone that ever underestimated me — and there'd been a few — did. I continued where I had been interrupted, only now there was venom in my voice. I had to fight to control my anger.

'You still haven't moved. This is your last chance. I've told the other lads to move and they have, now it's your turn.' Both looked from the dance floor to me and then back to the dance floor in a fit of arrogance. We were playing the game. I was throwing challenges with ambiguous speak and they were returning them with ambiguous body language. I made sure that my lead, left hand, my protective 'fence', was in operation so that I could control the very little distance that I had. In real situations — not to be mistaken for those created in the dojo where space is in abundance and people fence with legs and play at combat — we usually have about 18 inches to play with. This is the natural fighting distance, conversation range, where violence starts. It is not a distance that we choose, rather it is one that we are given. Whilst a favourable distance cannot always be chosen in the street the one that we are given can be controlled with a physical, verbal or psychological fence. The physical fence is a lead hand, or a utensil like a chair or a table, a verbal fence is a firm to aggressive command and a psychological fence is reputation or gait. If no fence is in operation we often lose the vital 18 inches and end up brawling on the floor, rolling over spilled beer and broken glass and getting kicked in the head by everyone with a grudge against doormen. I never operated without a fence. I controlled the range with my left hand, placed in between me and the two men as though I was using my hands to underline my speak.

The air grew thick and tense. I had given them an order and if they didn't move then the fight was on. I didn't really want to fight with these people unless I had to so I was desperately trying to give them as many chances as I could. In reality I knew that no matter how many chances they were given they'd abuse the lot and force either capitulation or a fight. I knew that this was going to become physical, but I still had to go through the ritual to satisfy myself that there was no other way.

'Yea, yea. We'll move in a minute.' This was another delaying tactic. I was getting fucking tired of the game, and, deciding to bring it to an end, I played my ace card.

'You either move now or you're going!'

The bird with the lip was already lined up — the first wrong move and he was off the planet. I'd hit him so hard his brain would think it was a cabbage — if it didn't think that already. I was beginning to wonder whether these two genius' had suffered brain death at birth. I still wasn't sure whether to 'go'. Physical didn't feel right. They were mouthy yes, but not over the line, not completely anyway. Every doorman has an invisible line that he keeps, and anyone who steps over that line is in for a 'bang'.

The problem is, professional troublemakers have an irritating habit of treading on the line but not over it. So they cabbage you but not enough for you to warrant doing anything about it. What you have to do with these people is either tempt them to step over the line so that your course of action is clear or let them go, and live with the fact that they have 'trod on your line'. The latter people you place to the back of your mind, you keep a record of them so that should ever come near you again and dare even to touch the line you can eclipse them without a second thought. Does that sound like overkill? It wouldn't if you had to deal with these arrogant bastards. It only sounds like overkill to those who have never experienced violence — but then to them everything is overkill, until some dude with an attitude treads on their life and they can't deal with it because they're shocked out of their pants.

'Were not going anywhere,' he said as though he couldn't believe that it had actually been suggested. Their sardonic, know-it-all grins were the same as I'd knocked off the faces of hundreds before them, they just didn't know how close they were to getting a battering.

So, what were my options here? I was on the very edge of a fight situation with two bombastic punters who had, through a series of body language and ambiguous speak told me that they thought I was a piece of shit. I could have swallowed and let them stay where they were. After all, no one would have really known, except me of course. No good. If I let them stay then they'd have been running the club and not me, next thing you know they'd be pouring their own drinks and taking money off the customers. Within days the word would have been out that the Buster's doormen were an easy touch and we'd have attracted vagabonds to the club like flies to shit. It wouldn't be the first nor the last time it had happened in this fair city.

I could have gone for reinforcements. I could have, I should have and with a bit more maturity I probably would have. As it was I was still a novice doorman with much to learn. I was still controlled by my ego and scared that calling for reinforcements would be a loss of face. 'Oh had to get you mates did you? Couldn't handle it yourself?' That sort of scenario was just too much for a ripe young ego like mine to bear. I could have physically dragged them out of the club by the scuffs of their necks. No good either. Most restraints are about as useful as a thong to an incontinent. Restraints are good against one person who is not too much trouble or who doesn't see you coming. No good against a man who wants to have a fight or two men who don't want to be restrained. These kind of techniques only work on police self defence courses with compliant partners who help you apply the technique. As far as I was concerned the only safe restraint in this trade was unconsciousness and that wasn't far off the way these guys were going.

I could have started attacking and hit everything that moved. After all, that's what a lot of doormen would have done. The threat was enough to spark many a brain shy. Not yet. Not for me, anyway. Maybe soon but not yet. Before I employ the use of a physical response there needs to be one vital ingredient in place: justification. If that isn't there I don't do the job, I can't do the job. And justification is a funny old thing. You could be in a group of four or five people, all of whom might not see justification, but you do, you see it as clear as day, and as long as you see it that's enough. Violence is not about having to justify your actions to others, it is about having to justify it to yourself. As long as you can do that then you can look yourself in the mirror and sleep at night. Having said that, and this might sound a little contradictory, you do have to be able to justify your actions to the law if you want to keep yourself out of jail for any length of time. But that is more about changing the way you tell it as opposed to the way you do it — if you see what I mean.

Justification was not far off, but it wasn't there yet. I needed more. To get myself more I grabbed the drink in the right hand of the man closest to me. He violently pulled his hand back so that I couldn't take it, beer spilling onto his shirt as he snatched.

'Get your fucking hands off me!' His backing glare challenged me to move — I was definitely in the mood for a challenge.

BANG! That was it. I'd heard enough and collected all the justification points, and more, that I needed. I hit him hard with a right hand that sent him spiralling backwards like a novice on a skating rink. He wasn't out, not yet anyway. Before he could recover his senses, he did look shocked, and just as I went in for the finish, John — who had come from the door to see why I had been so long — grabbed him around the neck in a vice like choke. My punches landed on his face bursting it up as John held him. John gave me one of those looks that said STOP, so I did.

The second bird came up from behind me with a heavy beer jug.

'That's my fucking mate you're hitting,' he said as he closed the gap. Obviously can't hide anything from this genius.

BANG!! Before he could get close to me with the glass, the most common edged weapon used in bar assaults and responsible for more plastic surgery than bears thinking about. I spun and hit him with one of those John Wayne type punches that knocks cowboys over and through tables and chairs. I launched him. He must have travelled five feet backwards; someone said that they thought he was on skates. He collapsed in a bloody heap in the corner — minus his front teeth.

I didn't make the connection very well and there was a gaping hole in the middle finger of my right hand, little bits of broken teeth floated around in the blood and after we had dragged the two guys from the club and left them lying on the pavement outside like they'd fallen from a great height, I cleaned up my throbbing, bloody hand, an injury that was to give me plenty of grief over the next few years. I heard the next day from a friend that 'gums' had to spend the next morning in the dentist chair having a plate fitted. I thought, rather un-Christianly, that with the amount of work I'd been sending them lately I should ask for a commission. Perhaps not.

My thoughts then and now are that it was all so avoidable. If they'd only had the humility to move to a different part of the bar. For the sake of a few feet one lost his teeth, the other lost his consciousness. Every time 'gums' looks in the mirror he will remember me, and don't try and convince the guy that I am a good man because he won't have any of it — even though he secretly knows he was in the wrong. Do you feel sorry for the lad? Don't. Remember who and what he was — a bully. The kind of boy that intimidates your child in school and makes his young life a misery, and perhaps bullies him so much that he has a breakdown or even commits suicide. It happens. He's the man that bullies your husband in the work place, fills his daily life with anguish. He's the boss that intimidates your wife or your sister in the office and makes her cry, no one dares to stand up to him, and eventually he forces her to pack in work. He's the guy on the factory floor that worries your brother so much that he has a breakdown, that breakdown has a profound effect on his life and smashes his marriage like china.

Bastards, low life wankers like this, change peoples lives for the worse, so please, don't feel sorry for him. All I did was give the guy a little bit of karma, I may have even helped him, showed him the errors of his ways as it were, steered him in a new direction. Every time a bully like this stands before me and wants to 'dance' I do my very best to oblige. I pay him back for every bad deed he ever slapped on a nice person that was too scared to fight back, and when I go to bed at night I sleep like a baby, I even feel good about what I did because I innately know it was right.

3. The Man who couldn't be Knocked Out

Twenty inches of neck, attached to a freakish body — the likes of which are not usually seen outside the pages of a *He-man* comic — with tree trunk legs and splaying arms carrying invisible buckets of water walked into Buster's night club. He paid for his entrance and thudded towards the bar barging through anyone who stood in his way. The man was a walking truck that liked to play professional Rugby and eat babies. John 'Awesome' Anderson made a mental note as he walked past. Instinct told him that he'd be fighting with this man before the end of the night. Sometimes you can just tell. C, another rugger player of six two and 210lbs approached John.

'Know who that is?' he asked John.

John drew on his cigarette and felt the adrenalin warm in his stomach. He shook his head as though to say 'don't know — don't care' though he knew he was going to be told all the same.

'That's Trevor. A fucking monster on the rugger field. He's the man that can't be knocked out.'

John raised his eyebrows as though to say 'now there's a challenge'.

The incident in the last chapter, dealing with bullies off their territory, is by no means isolated. Many, many times during my stint on the door I was to witness the demolition of one or more of these lowlifes. And I have to say that, as much as I abhor violence, I enjoyed seeing every one of these bastards hit the deck. People like Trevor were, in a way, bouncers' bogey men. People who didn't care how well you fought, how strong your rep, how big you were or even if you had a face like ten boxers, they wanted to fight you. In short they thought so much of themselves that they were not intimidated, not in the least, by any doormen. Their sole intention in life seemed to be in intimidating doormen, and often they succeeded. This was the absolute worst type of all because all the concepts we used for avoiding a physical response — avoidance, escape, dissuasion, loopholing etc — were exhausted before we even started. The short and the long of it was, and is, these wankers wanted to fight you and you either fought back or you abandoned ship. You had a choice, be the hammer or the anvil.

I remember well the incident with old '20 neck', the rugger player that couldn't be knocked out, because he was the epitome of every villain, of every bully that every doorman in the country, ney the world had faced at least once in their career. On the night club scene 20neck was pretty famous and on the rugger field the lad was a fucking legend. He frequented most of the city night clubs and intimidated the punters and the door staff wherever he went. As with many Rugger players, no disrespect intended to the nicer players out there — there must be one or two at least — this guy liked a drink and liked a fight, usually in that order, and was the most frightening and intimidating person in the western hemisphere (or at least in Coventry). If you asked every doorman to draw their own personal nightmare customer I bet the majority would draw a photo-fit of this lemon.

Have you ever watched *The Mask* with Jim Carey? With the huge villain who steals Carey's mask towards the end of the film? That's what '20 neck' looked like. He was 17 stone and fit with cauliflower ears — the result of hard play on the field — that could win prizes at a vegetable show. Oddly enough his brain could probably win prizes at a vegetable show too. Whilst he had a rep for fighting mostly he didn't have to because he frightened the living shit out of everyone just with his looks and demeanour. Every city has a meat head like this one but not every city has an 'Awesome Anderson' that can put giants to sleep quicker than lead behind the ear.

'20 neck' was stood at the bar like he'd paid the rent, he was with a few of his 'cling-ons' — less like the aliens in *Star Trek* and more like the bits of shit that hang from a cow's arse. Everyone in the room hated him and all stood in fear of what he was capable of doing. He'd destroyed more innocents in this city than I care to remember and we all hated the very ground that he walked upon. I wasn't working this particular night but as the story goes '20 neck' started playing up, intimidating other customers and stealing their drinks. He also refused to pay for beer that he had ordered and consumed and kept touching up the female customers, you know, the usual rugger player crack. He'd also butted a lad by the bar for getting served before him. After several complaints a couple of the doormen had gone to the bar to try and sort the situation out. When they told '20 neck' he had to leave he just laughed in their faces and said,

'Whenever you're ready to get me out just let me know.' The lads were a little psyched out I have to say. Colin said that it would take a fork lift to move this man monster whose head looked like a big square lump of granite sat on RSJ shoulders.

Unsure where to take the situation from here one of the boys went to reception for John and filled him in on the details. John already knew that he was going to be fighting so he took off his jacket and made his way to the bar. Muscles that you don't get out of the catalogue rippled through the white cotton sleeves, looking like they were going to burst at the biceps.

'Why haven't you got rid of 'the problem' Colin?' John asked as he paced towards the bar. Colin thought for a second.

'Well, he just said that he wasn't going.'

'You boys should have dealt with it.' he continued without looking at Colin. 'Too late now. I'll deal with it.' John spoke as though he was talking about an overdue bill or some inanimate puzzle that had to be resolved. They knew they should have dealt with it themselves but they'd allowed '20 neck' to dominate and had been psyched out as a consequence. It happens. That's what the head doorman is there for. The buck stops with him. I don't know a single doorman that hasn't at some time or other been psyched out by a person or situation like this. '20 neck' stood twice as wide as John, well twice as wide as every man in the room actually.

He smirked when John approached as though to say 'this is your head man?!' He made one of those smarmy smiles that says 'you've got more chance of moving a mountain.' He made the same mistake that many big men had with John. In clothes he looked pretty ordinary, inconspicuous. Stocky, but not so much so that you'd take notice.

Underneath was a different matter: the man was hugely muscular with rippling biceps and a back that was layers deep. He could bench press 400lbs and curl in excess of 220. Add to this the fact that John could punch like a pro boxer and had an iron will, forged from the adversity of several hundred encounters with the city's best and worst and you had a bundle of woe if you crossed his path. John was all 'pain and maim' — you know the scenario. '20 neck' had definitely read the cover wrong on this baby, all wrong.

'So what's the problem then?' John's voice was emotionless and to the point. He drew back on his cigarette and flicked it at the feet of '20 neck'.

'I don't got a problem. The problem is all yours.'

'I think you'd better leave.'

'I'm not leaving and you're not big enough to make me.' He smiled and turned back to his beer as though he rated John so little that he didn't even warrant eye contact. All eyes were on John and the space that he occupied. Everyone at the bar area stopped to watch the spectacle. John hid the effects of adrenalin with expert ease. He leaned back onto his right foot and tapped his left foot to the beat of the music; this hides the adrenal shake in the major thigh muscles that tells an observant opponent you're 'feeling it'. He gripped his voice and talked in low controlled tones to hide the voice quiver that spells panic from a hundred yards away. On the outside he looked like a rock, immovable and undaunted. John was a master of the 'game' and working on the premise that when ignorance was mutual confidence was king.

Inside, I know, he was feeling it the same as every man who ever had a fight. His arse hole would have gone from the size of a sixpence to the size of a dustbin lid. His adrenalin would have been rushing around his veins like a Formula One race car at Brands Hatch. His inner opponent, the voice of instinct, would have been gnawing away telling him to flee for his very life from this pre-historic beast. Most people watching would have seen a head doorman telling a freak-neck to leave the premises; when I watched John I looked deeper because I had stood in this man's shoes and faced many monsters just like the one he faced now. What I saw was a captain of self control, a man with the strength to over-ride his own instincts to 'run like fuck', and not only that but to be as cool as as snowman's bollocks in the process.

Our natural instinct as human beings is not to stand and fight, it is to run. Whenever you feel the urge to run away don't ever beat yourself up and think yourself a coward, you're not. We all feel like running away because that is how nature made us. The adrenal syndrome, a little antiquated for this cosmopolitan society, is man's safety mechanism, in-built to help us survive attacks from pre-historic beasts that were far too big and strong to stand and fight. Nature therefore gave us the instinct to run and only fight when no other option was available. The adrenal syndrome was far better suited to the mortal conflict of fighting or escaping the sabre toothed tiger, because running from him was not only wise it was also the only safe option. The concept of 'run for your life' is often lost in a decade where confrontation is not quite so tangible and 'legging it' may not be the answer (even though it is still the instinct that you feel). The confrontation may well be one you are expected to face, like a board room meeting, high mortgage rates, a row with the wife or a moron in a night club with a 20" neck who will take over the whole place if you don't 'stay'. As a night club doorman one cannot afford to go with natural instinct because you are being paid to 'stay'.

Anyway, I digress: this all confused '20 neck' who was still trying to master the art of eating, drinking and stringing sentences together. Every other mortal that he had dealt with in the past had worn their fear like a thorny crown. This baby — John — was different. He displayed no outward signs of fear, in fact he looked as though he didn't give a monkey's fuck. This display of control slightly un-nerved the man with a weetabix brain but he over-rode it and played the game right back.

Every man and woman at the bar seemed to hold their breath in unison, anticipating the battle that must surely ensue. They had never seen anyone stand up to this bullying monster before and, though they wanted to see his blood spilt, they found it hard to believe that he was beatable.

John knew before the approach that, by reputation, the guy was going to need careful handling. He had demolished many good men in the city and was a bouncer's nightmare. His pre-fight strategy had to be played just right if he was going to take this fuck brain off the planet. He already knew that an amicable settlement was an impossibility and that violence was well and truly 'on the cards'. But that was John's game. What he had learned over the years and what he knew was this:- the art of winning a fight was not in what physical tools one employed — though John did enjoy much success with his cannonball left hook and that only added to his confidence should a fight 'kick' — rather it was about pre-fight strategy, the 3 seconds before physical combat. The man that understood and controlled this baby the best was going to be the man that walked away with the accolades — in this case the scalp of '20 neck'.

'He hit that guy over there John,' Colin interrupted John's thoughts for a second and pointed to a battered and bruised youth a couple of feet further down the bar. John approached him through the crowd of customers, all of whom who were now looking on. U2, the popular Irish band, smashed out *Sunday, Bloody Sunday* in the background. They couldn't have known how apt their lyrics were.

'What happened?' John asked as he looked at the lad, eye closing, mouth bleeding, just a nice young chap out for the night with his lady. Not a fight in him.

'I don't know really, I got served before him and he just went mad. Butted me and punched me then kicked me in the head when I fell. I can't do nothing about it — look at the size of the guy?' he motioned towards '20 neck' who smiled as he looked at his handiwork.

John had been bullied at school, incredibly, and he felt really sorry for this youth before him, saw a little of himself there as a younger man. He was angry now. He turned back to '20 neck' knowing what had to be done. He walked back through the crowds who parted for him like he was a visiting dignitary.

'I think you'd better make your way out of the club mate.' As he spoke he grabbed the left hand of '20 neck' with his own right hand and gave a gentle tug as though trying to take his glass away from him. In reply '20 neck' violently yanked his hand away.

John was using the speak and the pull to test the waters, to gauge the response of the man before him. He had long since taken note of the half empty beer mug in his hand and knew from the many glassings that he had witnessed in the past just what damage a piece like that could do in the hands of intent.

'You want me out you take me out!'

The interview was over. They stared into each other's eyes for what seemed like a lifetime, the air was electric and the circle of people around them widened in anticipation of the inevitable affray. They wanted to spectate, but not be so close as to 'catch one' should a loose cannon fire in their direction. What John had gauged from the speak and the pull were two things; firstly, in these split seconds he had evaluated that the guy was not going to leave without a fight — it had to be a fight because he was too big and strong to try restraints, and secondly that when the glass in his right hand was touched he pulled back to his own right, this opened a window for a left hook — he liked left hooks.

John went for the glass again and used the same speak to hide his intent and engage the brain of his opponent. Engaging the brain wasn't a problem, this was a guy that still scratched his head at the milk on the doorstep every morning 'Uh! Who left that there?' This time he allowed a little hesitancy deliberately to creep into his voice to disarm his man mentally and spurn a millisecond of over-confidence that would open a bigger window for the attack that he intended to employ.

'You've got to go, mate.' As the words left his lips John moved his right hand forward as though trying to take the glass again. As before '20 neck' sharply pulled back to his own right.

BAAANGG!! It was a short left hook that travelled so fast it almost landed before it was thrown. It was so quick that a lot of the people didn't even see it, and because Colin was standing so close to John when he fired the punch many of the punters thought it was his and not John's. Colin said nothing to convince them otherwise. The left hook probably only travelled 6 inches; the connection was one of the most violent on record and the meat head hit the floor at a hundred miles an hour. In LA it might have measured on the Richter scale. He fell like a slaughtered cattle, his head smashing into the beer-sticky carpet where his feet were just a second before. His big face shuddered and he was in sleepsville. He hit the floor so hard that the beer glasses bounced off the three nearest tables and the punters who had just purchased them lunged forward to catch them as they tumbled through the air.

One of them said afterwards that he thought it was, and I quote, 'a fucking earthquake!' The whole club fell silent like a room of mannequins for what seemed like minutes and then, incredibly, as one they broke out into a rapturous, spontaneous applause that lasted for about twenty seconds. This guy (and people of his ilk) was hated so much that people were actually applauding because of his demise. Incredible. All eyes went to the floor then back to John who refused to let a smile hit his lips even though he was smiling from ear to ear on the inside.

The monster now looked like a sleeping baby. Blood gushed from his face where John had smashed his side teeth through his cheek. It needed twenty stitches to put it back together. John looked at the awestruck doormen. Colin smiled sheepishly.

'He's leaving now then, John.'

'Get that piece of shit out of the club,' John replied. As he walked to the door he looked back to see the three doormen struggling to move the big, unconscious rugger player. He was just too heavy. One of the lads, using a little initiative, moved all of the chairs and tables out of the way to create a make shift runway and the three of them rolled '20 neck', like a barrel, out of the exit door and onto the pavement. John couldn't suppress a smile. He lit up another cigarette and mentally rehearsed his statement for the police should they arrive. As far as I can ascertain this one incident retired '20 neck' from his intimidating ways — I'm glad, the fewer people there are like this one the better.

As you can see with this altercation it was the mastery of pre-fight that brought John the accolades. This is where it's at. Previously I had spoken to John many times about the reality of combat and the 3 second fighter and he was amazed that more martial artists had not cottoned onto the pre-fight philosophy that was so imperative to the winning of a confrontation. I tried to explain to him that most trained fighters had never fought outside the controlled arena and did not appreciate that there were different kinds of fighting. All they ever usually engaged in was controlled match fighting that disallowed any kind of grappling and restricted its players mostly to straight punches.

The freestyle revolution, instigated by many greats like the Alfie Lewis, Bob Sykes and Peter Consterdine had gone some way to redress this balance by allowing more contact and more variance in technique, even down to allowing throwing technique — but even there ground fighting was still a no-no. With many martial arts types fighting is performed in the controlled arena, at a manufactured range. It all starts with the touch of gloves or the bow of heads; basically that makes it match fighting and with so many restrictions that it does not even resemble real fighting. It is just an aesthetic dance. Fighting in the street is a far cry from this, it is also a far cry from match fighting even though, I have to say, match fighting is an honourable, though dying art.

Fighting, the real variety, breaks down into three categories. Firstly, match fighting, where two guys meet on the common and have an arranged fight, which usually always ends up in ground fighting. Secondly, ambush fighting, which is where you are rushed unexpectedly and have no fore-warning that a fight is about to occur. Usually the first indication of an ambush is a punch in the head — if the attacker is experienced it will be the the last you know of it too and you are likely to wake up attached to tubes and machines in the local hospital, or worse still end up in the obituary column. Then there is the 3 second fight where the physical is preceded by dialogue entrapments that act as the ultimate primer for assault.

The enemy of today is not a match fighter, that noble art died with my father's generation and takes balls — today's fighter just ain't got any of that rare commodity. Then there is ambush fighting. To the uninitiated who are not aware and do not understand the contemporary arena every fight will probably be an ambush because their heads are out there with Pluto and they wouldn't notice the build up to a scrap if you sent them a telegraph stating the time and place. 3 second fighting? This is where it is at today with the present enemy and you know what really fucking amazes me? A lot of the people that I try and pass this important message on to will not have any of it. Isn't that just fucking shocking? They don't believe me, but then why should they, I have only been involved in 300 fights so what do I know?

Sir Winston Churchill said that many men stumble upon the truth and then get back up and walk away as though nothing happened. You know why that is? Because the truth is just too simple, or it might mean too many changes or it simply isn't palatable. It just doesn't hold the mystique of ancient martial arts where the only thing addressed is the physical response — or certainly what is left of these honourable arts anyway. Combat is not — I repeat NOT — about hap-hazardly engaging in a physical response, or waiting to be attacked so that you can block and counter attack because 'spontaneity is the order of the day'. That's all bollocks and the people that sell it, bless them, are misinformed theorists whose only experience of combat is in the safe imagination of their own mind. What it is about is control before power, control is in the pre-fight and not the in-fight. But please, don't take my word for it read Sun Tzu, read Napoleon, read Musashi. These babies knew just what it was all about and their whole lives were based around warfare.

The street fighter's leading technique is not a kick or a jab, it's dialogue, words that are used to prime you and prepare you for the beating of your life. Most people are out of a fight before they even realise that they are in it because they are ignorant to the pre-fight ritual. Running parallel with this deceptive speak is an innate body language that I call attack ritual and if you understand this ritual you get a countdown before attack. John knew his enemy like a game hunter knows the Tiger. That, respectively, is what takes him and other doormen of his ilk safely through hundreds of encounters without experiencing a loss.

4. Alternative Night

Tuesday night at Buster's was alternative night and everyone with a fetish for dress, attitude and make-up would turn up to strut their stuff. It was always an incredible sight to behold. To make their night as trouble free as possible we, the door staff, would disallow any punter from entering the club if they looked too normal. Regular people, or townies as they were known, always seemed to end up causing trouble with the alternatives so, just to keep the peace, they were barred on Tuesday nights. This was important because the alternatives brought in a lot of money for the club and if they didn't get the place to themselves they would simply stop coming and find somewhere more select to spend their money.

When I first started working on alternative night it was a good laugh, men dressed as women, women dressed as men, men dancing with men and women with women, punks, freaks, drop-outs, druggies; you name it, we had them. After a while though, when the novelty of playing 'spot the tranny' (transvestite) wore off, it became a boring night with shite music that we all hated. It got so bad that 'Radio Rental' Rob used to plug toilet paper in his ears to block out the sounds that these people raved too. Luckily, alternatives very rarely caused trouble. It was not, it would seem, their way. I was glad about that because more often than not you couldn't tell the men for the women and when you could you often didn't want to touch them for fear of catching something — some of them were as scruffy and dirty as fuck with chains and hooks hanging from their ears and noses, and other places that couldn't be seen and shouldn't be mentioned.

It's OK to dress the way you like but I don't think there is any excuse for being dirty. I asked a lad one night why he didn't keep on top of his personal hygiene (I actually wanted to say 'why are you such a smelly bastard?'). He said that I should judge him by what is on the inside and not what is on the outside and that an enlightened person would not be put off by an outward appearance. What a load of bollocks! That's just a lazy man's excuse not to wash and shave every day. You don't have to wear designer clothes, just fucking wash once in a while. Give the world's nose a day off.

On alternative night even going to the loo could prove a troublesome affair. I remember one night when 'Radio Rental' went for a piss only to come tearing back out again, with a frightened look emblazoned across his mush. Apparently he'd just 'unzipped' by the urinals when a tall, leggy good looking woman — turns out it was a tranny — strolled in, plopped her hand bag on the sink next to the urinals, hitched up her skirt and proceeded to whop her dick out and take a piss. Poor Rob was goggle-eyed; he didn't know whether to laugh or cry. Tuesdays were notorious for attracting gay men and women, and sometimes people who were on the fence as it were.

One particular night, right at the end of the evening when we were clearing the club, Rob noticed a young male student hanging around the women's toilet. Not such an unusual occurrence on alternative night considering that the men and women were often hard to discern. What brought him to Rob's attention was the fact that he was pacing outside the ladies' looking at his watch as though impatient for someone to exit.

'You OK mate?' Rob enquired.

'Oh yea, fine. Just waiting for my girlfriend. She's been in there a while and I want to go home.'

Rob looked at his watch. It was 02.05.

'I'll give it a few minutes,' said Rob, 'and if she isn't out I'll go in and look for her. She's probably shouting 'Huighy' down the pan. She'll be OK.'

The lad smiled and Rob continued on his walkabout getting people to see their beers off and leave the club. At 02.15 the lad was still waiting impatiently outside the ladies' when Rob walked past for the umpteenth time.

'Sorry mate you're gonna have to make your way out. It's way past closing time.'

The lad, a nice looking smart kid, looked frustrated. He took a sharp intake of breath.

'You couldn't do us a favour, could you, and look in the ladies' for my girlfriend?'

Rob looked surprised. He'd forgotten all about her.

'She's not still in there, is she?'

'Yea. It's been twenty minutes now. I'm getting a bit worried about her.'

'Leave it to me. I'll check it out.'

At this Rob entered the ladies. If you think that men's toilets are bad you want to see the state the women leave theirs in. Make-up everywhere, sanitary towels on the floor, lewd comments on the walls written in make-up. A fucking shitty affair I have to say. When Rob walked in he noticed that someone had written on the mirror in dark red lipstick: it said, 'My mum made me a lesbian!' Underneath in blue lipstick someone had replied, 'If I give her the wool, will she make me one?' Someone else had written above the towel dispenser, obviously a feminist, a lesbian or a right ugly cow, 'Women need men like a heavy period on a tropical holiday'. Nice girls?

Rob looked around the small loo. No one to be seen. Of the three cubicles all were open and empty bar one. From inside the cubicle Rob could hear the low hum of a womanly moan. 'Must be ill,' he thought.

He was intrigued. He lent an ear to the door to hear better. He heard the moan again. The door wasn't locked so he gently pushed it open to see what was amiss. To his astonishment and amusement he did not find a woman moaning and wretching down the loo because she had drunk too much — he saw a woman, the young lad's girlfriend, sat on the toilet, knickers down and legs akimbo with another young woman kneeling between her legs 'scuba diving'. The moans were of ecstasy and not discomfort. Neither of them saw Rob and were too entwined to notice.

Rob said later that the girl on the loo probably had the cleanest genitals in the world because she had a woman in twice a week. He gently closed the door so that they didn't notice him and then shouted, trying to hide his embarrassment,

'Can we have the toilets empty now? It's time to go.' Then he quickly exited the toilets. He walked back outside the ladies', still marvelling at what he had seen. He had forgotten all about the young lad waiting for his girlfriend.

'Is she coming, then?' asked the lad, who couldn't have known how aptly worded his question was. Rob thought for a second and couldn't stop a sheepish grin from spreading across his face.

'Yea,' he replied, 'in a funny kind of way she is.'

The only alternatives that we did have any kind of physical with on the night club scene were the punk rockers, as they liked to call themselves at the time. A lot of these people looked like they were after winning awards for being dirty scruffy bastards; others were dead sweet and wouldn't hurt a fly.

Tony, the head, was at the bar in Buster's waiting to get served on this particular evening. He was visiting the club with his lovely wife, Betty, who was small enough to fit into Tony's pocket, for a quick drink before he went on to work at one of the other clubs in the city. The bar was pretty busy and there was a fair bit of pushing and shoving going on to get drinks. This is only to be expected in a busy club. The first push Tony felt he ignored, 'it's all part and parcel of the night club scene' he told himself.

The second push, far more blatant this time, was superceded by some foul language that made him turn to see the bearer of the sewer expletive. It was a tall punk rocker with leather biker trousers and a black, cap sleeved T shirt that showed off his muscular upper arms. The guy with him, dressed similarly, looked pale and snotty like he had just taken his head out of a bag of glue. Both looked pretty detached with wide eyes and aggressive gaits. Tony ignored the pair and turned back to the bar only to be pushed once more by the tall punk. Tony turned and faced him. As he did so, Betty, who knew from experience where this was all heading, pulled his arm.

'Leave it, Tony,' she said.

'It's all right love. No problem.' He said it in the gentle way that he always spoke to Betty. He idolised her and treated her like a little doll even though she did have a twenty stone temper on her. Tony upset her one day at home and stormed out of the house; he was about twenty yards down the road when he heard CRAAASH!!! As he turned to see what the racket was a heavy glass ashtray — one he recognised as his own — landed inches from his feet. She'd thrown it at him from the kitchen, clean through the window. Had he have been walking a little slower he might have been wearing it in the back of his head. Another friend of mine's wife, in similar circumstances, threw a tea mug at him so hard that it stuck in the plaster on the wall next to his head. Women!

'Listen mate, I know you want a drink. So do we. Take it easy and stop pushing. OK?' Tony stood sideways on and lined the tall one up with the head, just in case. Druggies were pretty fucking unpredictable and you had to be ready at all times.

'I never fucking pushed ya. Must be imagining things.' His tone was aggressive and challenging. Tony contemplated launching 'the head' but thought better off it. He knew that Betty wouldn't like it and he also had respect for the doormen that were working and didn't want to 'kick off' in their gaff.

'Well, just give me some space and everything will be sound.' Tony was polite but firm. The punks both stared hard at him and he knew that it was going to 'go'. He turned back to the bar and made himself ready for the next, inevitable push. These guys were all so fucking predictable. He could hear the punks giggling behind him and knew that they had mistaken his politeness for weakness. Tony wasn't weak, he was just clocking up enough justification point to enable him to work a little better. Tony was a bit like me, he needed plenty of justification before engaging in fisticuffs. Some of the lads need hardly any at all; they will 'go' an the first given opportunity.

Tony B recently had a big Irishman ask him 'what's a coon like you doing in a nice place like this?' BAANG!!!! He answered with a right cross that was heard before it was seen. The guy never opened his eyes for ten minutes and when he did he got instant serenity. PC, local gangster and money lender maimed for as little as eye contact, this in a volatile environment being construed as a subliminal challenge to fight. After knocking a local heavy out with a pummelling right, he sat astride the unconscious man's chest and awaited consciousness. Every time the man opened his eyes PC knocked him out again. He was knocked out five times before leaving him alone, and that was only because the pub had opened. Awesome Anderson was the same. If some one really upset him he'd wait until they came too from the first KO and then KO them again. It's a brutal arena that can't be taken too lightly.

Tony the head had just turned back to the bar when HUMPH! The tall muscular punk pushed his mate 'glue bag' flying into him. Tony turned angrily. Betty stood back, she could see that his justification bag was full to overflowing. She was a great woman, a doorman's dream, she knew exactly when to step in and when to step away.

My Sharon is just the same, if it goes she just stands back and takes notes. No sense in trying to stop a guy when his mind is made up, you'll only get in the way. The person that tries to hold you back usually gets you hurt because they tie up your arms and your focus, they distract you enough to get you killed. I always say to Sharon, 'if I 'go' don't come near me, just let me do it. If anyone else gets involved hit them with anything that comes to hand.' She's a good girl and has been at my side on many occasions when I've had call to teach a lesson. I remember beasting a local boxer who grabbed me around my arms when I tried to defend myself against a wild man in the club. After I battered the wild man I battered the boxer too. When he lay on the ground before me I told him, 'don't ever fucking touch me again.' No doubt he thought me a little 'over the top' but I know of many doormen who have been stabbed whilst someone held their arms to stop them fighting.

The tall punk stood back and splayed his arms cockily. He shrugged his shoulders.

'Accident!'

The onlookers had already moved back to make an arena for the trio. In a club like this fights were so common that they were almost seen as 'side shows'. The Monkees were blasting out *Cheer Up Sleepy Jean* above the cafuffle of several hundred chattering voices, laughing, joking, ordering drinks, all competing to get above the monotonous night club babble that stayed in your ears for hours after it had ceased.

BAAAANGGG!!!! Tony travelled over five feet with a flying head butt that sent the punk on a trip that no narcotic could ever send him. He hit the floor arse first and slid along the carpet for several feet, as though he were on a snow sled, knocking over a table full of drinks before coming to a halt in an unconscious heap. His face had grown a new feature, a nose, pissing blood, the size of Florida. Punk number two's eyes followed his mate as he slid the length of the bar, as his eyes shot back to Tony. BAAAANGGGG!!! He got the same and collapsed on the spot, also sporting a new nose. Tony turned to Betty,

'Sorry about that love. What do you want to drink?' She shook her head; being married to Tony she had witnessed more KO's than Harry Carpenter. But, to her, Tony would always be her gentle giant, even though he could 'butt' for England. The two punks were careful about who they chose to shove in the future, they learned their lesson well, 'fat men can fight'.

5. A Stitch In Time . . .

'Hey Dave, any chance of picking up the new Whitney Houston LP for me?' Dave was one of the regular DJ's at Buster's and very good he was too. He'd always looked after me whenever I wanted a record or album. He said he had a mate in the trade who could get them for next to nothing, which meant I always got them free. I was naive enough to think that this was because I was a good bloke and that Dave was a mate; I hadn't been at the club very long so I didn't know the real reason. I should have guessed really from giveaway signs like the love bites on the back of his neck but, as I said I was a little naive. Of course all the lads on the door knew Dave was gay but thought it funny not to tell me until it was almost too late. Let me give you a little background on 'gay DJ Dodgy Dave,' and night club DJ's in general.

Dave was your archetypal DJ who could never seem to switch off. Whether he was talking on the mike to 500 people in a busy night club or chatting in the street to one person, he was loud and cheery. Though he didn't notice it, he was a DJ 24 hours a day. His friends found it a little embarrassing, because even in normal conversation he was ever on the verge of announcing 'a great new record from a fantabulous new artist who does a lot for charity, but doesn't like to talk about it.'

He was a sensitive soul, so no one ever told him to shut the fuck up and give the rest of the world a chance. Dodgy Dave dreamt of becoming a Radio One DJ and, like every disc jockey in the world, was constantly sending demo tapes to radio stations and was in a constant state of 'limbo' awaiting the good news that never seemed to come. Sadly it never did and never will. At best Dave was a good night club DJ. His mood was determined by his radio station correspondence. When the demo tape was in the post he was high and inspired; when it was inevitably returned with the perfunctory refusal letter he was low and despondent. People were always telling him what a good DJ he was and he must have wondered why the powers that be in the top stations could not see his talent.

In the club, Dave was the eyes and ears of the doormen. As well as playing the tunes of the day, he also scanned the dance floor for trouble or its potential. He had a little panic button hidden in his box that he could press to alert the doormen 'if and when'. He was ever so slightly sycophantic towards the doormen — largely due to the fact that they scared the living shit out of him — and did every thing they asked without demure. Because he was an employee of the club and felt that he had the protection of the doormen, Dave could often be a little cocky and off hand with the punters, knowing that he only has to press the panic buzzer and we would come running to his aid. Of course we all noticed this weakness in him but turned a blind eye, protecting him even when sometimes he was in the wrong. The doormen all looked upon the staff in the club as family, if any one ever became physical with them, then we took it very personally.

An attack on the staff was as bad as an attack on us and we had a little golden rule: 'anyone touches a member of staff gets a battering'. The Chinese say that the best way to train a monkey is to slaughter a chicken in front of it — the best way to protect the staff from attacks is to destroy the first person who does it so that every other punter in the world says, 'don't fuck with the staff at Buster's — the doormen take it very personally!'

I learned this lesson early from Jock, one of the best doormen the city had ever seen. On my first night at The Tally-Ho he told me and the other doormen, 'anyone touches a doorman make an example'. We did and it worked well. We had very few instances of staff being abused. To us, it didn't matter if you were yellow, green, gay, lesbian or even fucking alien (some of the staff at Buster's were definitely bordering on it), we looked after our own in the same way as you would look after your own kin.

I remember some little wank upsetting my little sister Mariejo at work. He wandered into my night club one night and I thought all my Christmases had come at once. I cornered him by the bar and said,

'What's the crack with my sister? I hear you're upsetting her.'

'No, listen Geoff,' he said, as though we were best buddies, 'your sister's lying . . .'

WHACK!!

I'd heard enough. I rammed him up the wall by the throat until his wind pipe closed and sent gargling noises from his rapidly turning blue lips.

'Listen you little fucking pleb, you as much as look at my sister sideways again and I'll make your face into a fucking horror mask!' When I let go he fell to the floor choking. He never upset my sister again.

Dave wanted to 'get on' and often crept like a creepy thing around the management to meet this end. There was a lot of needle between Dave and the other resident DJ. Lets call him by an appropriate pseudonym, 'Slippery Deck', who felt that they had to compete with each other to win favour with the management. This was also another reason why he felt he had to keep in with the doormen as we had a big influence over what went on in the club. We always got the impression that Dave would really have liked to be a doorman — though he had more chance of getting pregnant — because he 'talked the talk', but really he was just a pussy. Whenever it did 'kick off' his nerve turned to jelly. When Dave worked there was always a heavy effeminate male influence around the DJ consul.

My mistake with Dave was being too nice. In some ways I would have been better off being like John and not letting anyone other than the other doormen close because, as was the case with Dave, familiarity breeds contempt. He used to fuck about and try play sparring with me and to be honest I didn't have the heart to knock him back. John was different, anyone tried to play spar with him and he'd grab them into his vice like grip and strangle them until they were nearly unconscious — they never tried again. This worked well for John but I found it difficult. I was an easy going chap who didn't like to upset people unless it was absolutely necessary; then when I did I'd usually go over the top.

Like the guy that strolled in the club one night, I knew him he was a nice person, or so I thought. When I saw him, I left John and Colin who were stood by the cloakroom in reception and went over to him at the paying-in desk,

'How ya doin'?' I said cheerily, putting my arm around his shoulder in a welcoming manner. I liked to make my friends feel welcome. So many doorman won't talk to you unless you're a 'face' or a 'name' and almost seem ashamed of their non doormen friends. What's that all about? That just shows weak character. My friend, my ex-friend, looked at the other doorman and then at me as though I was covered in shit, and slowly yet deliberately pulled my arm from his shoulder and placed it by my side. Then he looked back at the doormen again as though for appraisal and slapped the top of my head where the hair no longer grows.

'I'm..all...right!... How... are....you?' He said, timing each word with a slap. It was pretty fucking humiliating I can tell you. I just exploded. I grabbed his hand and swept his feet from under him, so hard in fact that he flew into the air for what seemed like minutes and then he landed heavily on the reception carpet. I threw my right hand, at speed, and stopped it right on his nose. I was almost foaming at the mouth. I seethed through gritted teeth,

'Have I got you? Have I fucking got you.' I think so. This wank showed no respect for me at all, even though I had given him plenty. I know I might have been a little over the top with the sweep but the way he made me feel he was lucky that I didn't really go over the top. I hate disrespectful people.

Now John was different, he never let people get close enough to take advantage and be disrespectful. To the uninitiated this might have made him seem mean and moody, not at all approachable, though we knew him better. He was the kind of man that felt saintly thoughts, though he shared them not, and enacted saintly deeds but did so as anonymously as possible — recognition embarrassed him greatly. His hard approach did have its drawbacks. John was born hard eyed and stone faced and whilst this might have helped him to scare the shit out of those who 'chanced their arm' (literally with John), it didn't always endear him those that didn't understand his 'way'; the ones that he didn't want to scare but, inadvertently did anyway.

If you ever have the privilege of meeting the man you may be surprised that he is not as big, physically, as you might think. He's only about five foot eight and his doorman apparel curtains his Herculean dimensions into the shadow of modesty. Usually he is laid back and occasionally, when necessary, colder than a December pudlock. John wasn't really the type of man to tell you when he liked you, he spoke with actions rather than the often sticky employment of words or sentiment. A head lock, a grab, a push, a friendly jab in the ribs were all, to John, ways of saying 'yea, you're alright'. And if he choked you out then you were really 'in'. John's tactile displays were of endearment from a man who found 'words' difficult. So, with John he would just hurt them once and then they wouldn't bother coming back again.

With me I let situations outgrow themselves until I had to do something serious to stop them — as in the case of Dave. It all started off as a bit of a joke, messing around, and gradually grew, until in the end Dave would belittle me in front of customers, which wasn't a great thing when you consider that I had to keep the respect of the clientele if I was going to inspire confidence. I was hardly likely to do that with a Gay DJ calling me names and offering me outside for a fight every other minute. Add to that, the fact that I found out in the meantime that he was gay and after my bum, and that he was not getting my records cheep but buying them for me, out of his own money, as little presents — I had a bit of a situation on my hands. First thing I did, of course, was to stop asking him to get me records; the infatuation had to end — I had the reputation of a woman's man to uphold. Secondly, I had to try and stop him messing around when I was working. What to him might have seemed a joke was to me an embarrassment and not because he was gay. Joking aside, that didn't bother me as I have had many gay friends over the years and was confident enough in my own sexuality to not feel threatened by it, like so many people do. It was the fact that he was starting to 'take the piss'. To be honest, I didn't really know what to do for the best. I asked John. He was no help at all: 'should have just knocked him out the first time he fucked about.' No grey areas with John.

The situation found its own solution at the very end of one Thursday evening when were just preparing to sit down for a staff drink. I was by the main doors of the club talking to the last of the customers as they were leaving.

BANG!!!

From out of nowhere Dave rushed past me, without warning or provocation, and back handed me in the 'family jewels', then ran off laughing. As a deep ache rocketed into my stomach my head went and by the time I caught up with the lad he was giggling by the DJ consul in the middle of the club. I ran at him with anger emblazoned across my face and swept his legs from under him with a big heavy double leg sweep that sent him high in the air. As he landed, crashing through a table and chairs, I lifted my right foot up and stamped on his head letting out a blood curdling KIAAA! I pulled the stamp on impact the way I have a thousand times in training. I stood above him almost foaming at the mouth. He curled up like a big fat ball and was yelping in pain. There was blood everywhere. 'Oh no,' I thought, 'I've killed the DJ.'

Half an hour later the lad was lying on a bed at the local hospital having eight stitches sewn into his head. Might add to his kudos to have a Heidleburgh scar. I was back at the club, still feeling angry but also feeling a little guilty. John, cracking a rare smile, was winding me up saying that we had had a 'lovers tiff', which didn't help my mood. He was also was telling me, through giggles, that it was my own fault for letting it go for so long. A stitch in time saves nine.

The manager approached me as I sipped on my half lager and crunched my lovely smoky bacon crisps, he seemed stern,

'Geoff, did you just put Dodgy Dave in hospital?'

I was going to give him the whole story of how Dave had pissed me off and embarrassed me but I thought 'fuck it', I wasn't in the mood. If he was going to sack me then so be it.

'Yea, That's right I did.' I said it without looking up. His face went from stern to smiling, he patted me on the back.

'Well done,' he congratulated, 'about time someone put him in his place.'

The whole table laughed. Needless to say I didn't get any more free records, but I didn't get any more abuse either.

6. Fat Men Can't Fight!?

How many times have you heard that old saying about fat people being unfit and not able to have a fight? What a lot of bollocks. I've worked with some fatties in my time, no disrespect intended to these portly fellows, and they have impressed the hell out of me. Fat or not these fellows 'could have a fight'. I'd like to start this chapter by apologising to any of my friends that I might mention who perhaps do not see themselves as being fat. I'll try and say it as quietly as possible in case any offence is taken. Bruce Lee, I'm a big fan, by the way, once said of an eastern master that had more chins than a Chinese telephone book, 'his chi must have sunk into his stomach'. In saying this he was kind of insinuating that because the guy was a fatty he couldn't have a fight. Well, Mr Lee, on this occasion we have to agree to disagree; I can only say that you obviously never worked with a fat guy.

What I would like to demonstrate in this chapter is that being overweight doesn't necessarily mean a fucking thing. Some of my best mates were/are dimensionally challenged and it never stopped them eclipsing normal thin people and it certainly never stopped them attracting a bevy of beautiful ladies.

If we are talking about overweight fighters I have to start with a legend, Tony the head. You may remember Tony from *Watch My Back* and *Bouncer*. I absolutely fucking loved the guy and, my goodness, could he have a fight. Tony had to be carrying twenty-two stone over a six foot frame with a large belly at the front and legs like tree trunks. His face was big also, but as charismatic as they come with scars running this way and that through his cheeks and eyebrows from several stabbings in some of the worst shit holes this side of 1920's Shanghai. He'd been stabbed by brothers, sisters, mothers and fathers in his time on the door. If we are talking about being stabbed, Tony is the metaphoric pin cushion.

Once, when restraining a youth in a night club in the centre of town, he felt a sharp pain under his right armpit and thought little more of it until he let the lad go and dropped his arm, only to find a stiletto blade sticking out of his ribs.

'I don't remember leaving that there?!' he said to his sidekick before collapsing on the floor.

Another time he opened the doors of a night club, long since closed down now because of the heavy volume of gratuitous violence, to be faced with a mad axeman, already in full swing with a rusty, heavy, wood chopping axe. Sure that this was to be his *coup de grâce*, because there was no way he could stop the axe from finding a bed in his skull, Tony closed his eyes and awaited the most dreaded finale. It never came. Only a heavy thud above his head. He carefully opened one eye and then the other only to discover that the axe had been swung so high and so hard that it had hit the top frame of the door and stuck fast. The wielder was swinging off the axe to try and release it so that he could 'try again'.

It turned out to be a guy that he'd thrown out earlier in the night. He tugged and pulled at the chopper — he was a black guy and you've heard the stories of how big a black guy's chopper is — and tried to pull it free. Tony, not one to miss such a golden opportunity, hit him with a headbutt that separated him from the axe — and terra firma — and sent him sprawling into the road like he'd been shot from a cannon. He lay, unconscious, in a blooded heap. The damage was so substantial that the ambulance driver later said he thought the guy had been the victim of a hit and run car accident.

The axeman lay motionless for the best part of twenty minutes before the ambulance actually came and scraped up his remains and took him off to hospital. They couldn't straighten his nose and said it looked as though it had been put through a blender.

As you have probably noticed Tony was a 'head' man. And a master thereof. He could headbutt with missile accuracy from as far away as six feet and as close as whispering in your ear. I never saw anyone survive the mighty wrath of a Tony R headbutt. He also taught me to use the head and, though it is not my main artillery technique, it is a favoured strike. I tend to use it spontaneously — ask any of my sparring partners — if the situation gives me the right openings.

I once had a war of a fight in sparring with a mate of mine, Barrington, a brilliant full contact player who currently (1996) holds the World Heavyweight Full Contact Crown. We'd been battling for about ten minutes during which I bashed him and he bashed me, no quarter was asked and none was given. He's a fucking tough man whom I respect very highly. He came in just a little too close and I dropped the head on him.

'He's fucking nutted me!' he laughed incredulously, then threw me over his shoulder with Ippon Shianagi. I jumped back up and we went at it again until we both stopped from exhaustion. Barrington is a rare fighter — one of the most respected doormen in the city — who can take it as well as he can give it.

I remember one night when I worked in 'The Parrot' night spot. I had to remove a lemon from the club because he was doing an impression of a rectum. I grabbed him from the back, one hand on each of his shoulders, and marched him from the club. All the way down to the front door the man abused me and told me what a wanker I was and that I'd regret throwing him out, you know the crack, same old scenario. I didn't react to the blurb because the guy was a lemon and drunk and didn't really need bashing. As I got to the door he got louder and louder and more abusive. He was starting to get on my tits a little. As we actually reached the door he placed his hands on either side of the frame and wedged himself so that I couldn't push him out. He turned his head to tell me that he 'wasn't going!' and a little window of opportunity presented itself.

BANG!! I hit him with a short headbutt, just as I had been taught — Tony would have been proud of me — just to shut him up really, I didn't intend the contact to be heavy. It was, and he hit the deck like an unconscious thing. I dragged him from the club and dumped him in the flower bed where he spent the next ten minutes. When he awoke, surrounded by flowers, he must have thought he'd reached the promised land.

A lot of doormen who don't work in the day take up unofficial jobs as minders for the 'kiters'. I did myself for about a year when the funds were lower than the third button on a snake's waistcoat (though if any policemen are reading 'I just made that bit up!') Basically, this entails following the girls or lads who spend on stolen credit cards and protect them should they get caught.

'C the crook' was the main man for kiting in this city — though, of course, he is a respectable citizen now — and took a team out every day of the week to spend on someone else's card. Not a good thing and I'm not proud of the fact that I was involved for a while, but let he who has not sinned cast the first stone. There are many people about who frown upon this 'criminality', but there are very few of us who haven't committed a crime at some point in our lives, and then rationalised it with weak justifications like, 'I don't mind having stuff from shops, they're insured for it', or, 'it's not really stealing, it's a perk of the job'. Don't kid yourself, whether you stole it or bought it from someone who bought it off someone who stole it, it's still stolen. My mate was horrified that I 'minded' for the kiters and yet he had no qualms about adding £500 onto an insurance claim that he had placed when his garage was burgled. That's stealing too, but he rationalised it by saying that 'everyone does it!' It doesn't matter if the Queen herself fiddles her insurance, he's still stealing £500. We all love to abhor crime but think nothing of buying something that is a little 'warm' because it's half price. Hypocrisy in our society knows no bounds it would seem.

On this particular occasion Tony was minding a young lady. She had gone into a superstore to spend on the card and had been sussed by one of the check-out girls who called a security guard to come and arrest her. Tony, never more than a few feet away from his charge, noticed the debacle and moved forward just as the guard, a hefty man in an ill-fitting brown security uniform (who walked around the store like he owned the fucking place) grabbed hold of the young lady. He held her arm with a vice-like grip that came from a breakfast of steroids and an evening ritual of weight training — which was great credentials for being a 'security' man but they could hardly have prepared him for 'the head'.

'Hey. That's my fucking wife, get your hands off her!' Tony shouted at the guard. The guard, not sure what do do now — this wasn't in the manual — turned to look at Tony.

BAANGG!! Tony launched the guy through the air with a butt and he landed in a display of Walkers Crisps (no more Mr Nice Guy!?) desperately trying to find his consciousness; it was hiding with his bottle under a bag of smoky bacon at the bottom of the pile. Tony and the girl legged it from the store leaving the guard 'in the crisps'.

Alex wasn't a bad lad, in fact when he was sober he was a nice bloke but, he could have a fight and when he'd drunk too much he could be a fucking nuisance. Because he was fond of the fists and the drink this made him a dangerous person. Fighters and drink mix a perilous cocktail that can explode when least expected. Tony realised this so, when Alex refused to leave the pub one night after drinking half of Coventry dry and abusing the bar staff like he was in a bar staff abusing contest, he was on his guard. Tony had asked him to leave more times really than he deserved and each time he asked, Alex got more and more abusive. He, like so many before him, made the fatal error of misreading Tony's respect for fear. He thought that Tony was scared of him and that he was 'just another fat doorman' and that's why he was asking so nicely. In fact Tony was asking nicely because that was his way — he liked to give people a little respect. He liked a drink himself and knew that, as Ju-Jitsu guru Dave Turton says 'not every dog that barks, bites'; they didn't all need a kick up the arse.

In short Tony was trying to give the lad a chance. There are only so many times that you can ask a guy to leave before you start looking like an absolute twat and lose face. We're not talking ego here we're talking 'face', respect. If the punters in the place you work don't respect you then you have no power and can't work. If you let people get away with too much too often every fucker in the world will be queuing at your door to take a shot at the title. This is probably the main reason why the iron lady, Mrs Thatcher, kicked some arse in the Falklands conflict: if she didn't 'make an example' every little country in the world with a chip on its shoulder and a point to make would have been chancing their arm.

Tony had asked Alex to leave more than half a dozen times and the rest of the people in the bar were starting to sit up and take notice. They knew that Alex was a handy lad, a local 'name' and were more than interested to see how Tony was going to handle the situation. It would act as a benchmark to how far they could push things in the future or whether indeed they could push things at all. By now Alex had his back rested to the bar and looked to all intents and purposes as if he had grown there. He was as arrogant as I have ever seen any man who didn't have a death wish.

'I'm not going anywhere and you ain't movin' me. No way!'

'Alex, don't be stupid, you've got to leave and you ain't makin' things easy for me. Now do me a favour and leave. Come back tomorrow and have another drink then.'

'You can fuck off. I'm goin' nowhere and you, you fat fucker, ain't gonna move me either.'

Tony closed the range slightly and contemplated dragging Alex out of the place forcefully but considered the risk to be too great. You don't try and restrain a guy who wants to fight because you'll just end up losing, especially when the guy is a 'face'. Tony touched Alex's hand to monitor his aggression and intent; Alex gave him the answer he was looking for by violently yanking his arm away.

'Don't fucking touch the merchandise unless you wanna buy.' This was another example of ambiguous street speak that really meant 'don't touch unless you are willing to fight for it'. Tony knew the speak, he was a fucking linguist and was as fluent in it as any I'd worked with it. He now had no other option open to him but to become physical so he started his priming. At this stage the reader may be thinking 'well there you go now, that doorman is going to hit this guy and there is really no need, he's just a drunk'. Of course, the lads that have been to the 'dance' know the steps and won't be thinking that at all, they'll be thinking 'fuck me, why's he taking so long. I'd have fired my first shot long since'. What I'd like to ask here is for those who are saying 'overkill' to give me a solution that might solve this equation, and then run that hypothetical solution to its natural conclusion. But be quick because hesitancy can prove fatal when facing a potentially violent man.

Here's a few alternatives that you might suggest:

1) You could gently grab his arm and try to walk him to the door. He's tried that and been warned that if he tries it again he is going to get a 'plum' eye. He'll pay the price. The price with a man like Alex could be anything from a bloody nose picked up in the scuffle to a glass in the neck or a fatal knife in the ribs. I've known them all happen to over-patient doormen.

2) He could ask the pub staff to help him get Alex out. The staff are not paid to do that, just the same as you are not paid to pour beer or collect glasses (do you know how many doormen have been attacked and hurt when they were carrying hands full of glasses — don't collect them, it's not safe). And an amateur at the wheel is likely to get badly hurt and probably abused in the aftermath by the guy that you are trying to throw out.

I remember one young barman who jumped in to help the doormen against a notorious gang, in a night club in the city. The gang saw him the next week out with his wife and battered him until his brain thought it was a cabbage. When his lady tried to stop them she got her teeth knocked out for her trouble. Bar staff are not equipped — even if they think they are — to do the job of a doorman. If they were they'd be working the door for £10 an hour and not behind the bar for £3. Does that make sense? Don't let them get involved for their own sakes. If I get trouble in the aftermath from some wanker that I've 'dealt' with who has a thirst for revenge then that's OK, I can handle that, it's my game, what I'm paid for and what I train every day of my life to do. These people don't, and won't, handle the trauma of the 2am phone call that says 'we are gonna kill your wife and kids'.

One barman I know had a gang after him for over a year for 'interfering'. They turned up at his day job, his house, where he drank. He never got rid of these parasites until he moved, through sheer terror, from the city. By that time his wife was on the verge of a breakdown and his life had become a living nightmare. They never chased the doormen that were involved, just the barman because they knew that the doormen were paid to do what they had done, the barman wasn't. Think about it.

3) Phone the police. Let them deal with it. That's a giggle. Bit like telling teacher really, isn't it? You lose more respect by calling the police than you would if the guy kicked seven kinds of shite out of you, at least then you could say you had a go. And what does it tell the people around you if you have to call the police because you have a troublemaker in the club? It tells them that you can't deal with the situation. You can't handle it. Why is the manager paying you £50 a night? So that you can call the police every time a situation scares you. He could fucking do that himself and save a few hundred pounds a week. Call the police and your name as a doorman will be shit within a few days. There is no honour in that solution at all. If the police are called it also affects the chances of you club/pub regaining its drinks licence each year when it goes up for renewal. The police will oppose it on the grounds

that they had to be called to calm trouble at the place on several occasions. The only time the police should be called is when you have a riot on your hands and it has completely outgrown the door staff — then the manager will call them all on his own. Even then I wouldn't call the police, I'd call someone that could 'deal' with it properly, if you see what I mean.

4) Let him stay. Yea, that' a good one, like hiring a gamekeeper who doesn't want to kill rabbits. He'd abused the bar staff, he has to go. You let him stay and you haven't done your job, you'll be out of work quicker than a vertiginous roofer, probably within days of starting and, again, your name will be shit as a doorman.

5) Knock him out? — now, that's a little closer to the mark. BANG!!! Tony hit Alex with a headbutt that was so fast and so powerful that the back of his head hit the bar directly behind him. In unison everyone in the bar said 'OHHH!!' as though it were their own heads being bounced off the polished oak. As he catapulted back up again, already 'out' and already oozing crimson, Tony caught him with a second butt that sounded like a willow bat hitting a cricket ball for six. He dropped to the floor in a crumpled heap. He was, as Tony said, restrained.

A week later Alex's head was still throbbing from the butt and he was still just getting used to his new nose — it quite suited him; gave him kudos though I'm sure he'd have liked a less painful way of acquiring 'character' than a twenty stone flying forehead in the face.

Drinking at another pub, one that he was not yet barred from, his mate approached unaware of what had happened to him at the Pippin.

'Why don't you drink at the Pippin any more, Alex?'

Alex took a painful sip of his beer through busted lips and thought for a second then replied,

'Ah, the beer there gives me a headache!'

Another time Tony, dressed as Santa during the Christmas period and giving out presents to the locals at the Pippin pub, was attacked by a guy with a previous grudge. When I looked over from the bar I almost choked on my smoky bacon crisps as I watched 'Santa' with this guy by the throat headbutting him all across the room. I promptly tore up my Christmas list, I can tell you.

Talking about fancy dress, and changing the subject slightly away from fatties, I remember the time three of the lads got dressed up for a night out on the town. They weren't going to a party or anything like that, they just wanted to dress up and have a laugh. There was Cash, he owned the Diplomat pub, and dressed up as a Lemon; Lee, a local doorman who'd worked some of the roughest establishments on record and had a rep as a good KO merchant — he dressed up as a banana, and Liam, one time DJ and all round nice guy, who was dressed up as an apple. The 'fruit salad' went from pub to pub in their fancy dress and had a great laugh.

After about an hour Cash left the other two and made his way back to the Diplomat to look after the bar — he was the manager after all — whilst Liam and Lee stayed for 'one more drink'. After another hour, and several more drinks, Liam and Lee also decided to make their way back to the Dip to finish off the evening. On their way, however, they ran into a little trouble. A group of lads that they passed along the route through the city centre started barracking them, 'you fucking pair of 'fruits', you Banana!' etc etc.

A fruit was streetspeak for a gay in Coventry so the lads were non too happy about the abuse. They'd drunk a bit too, so they shouted a bit of abuse back. The three men approached Lee and Liam and things heated up a little, resulting in Lee knocking one of the guys clean out. They legged it back to the Dip with plod heavily on their tails and hid themselves away in a corner of the pub. Half an hour later the police were at the door of the pub 'pursuing a complaint'. Kenny the bodybuilder was at the front door. He knew what had gone on but acted dumb.

'What can I do for you lads?' he asked politely, with his permanent 'joker grin' spread across his face from ear to ear.

The two policemen looked a little embarrassed, and the first one stuttered,

'We're looking for a couple of 'fruits'.'

Kenny felt an instant urge to split his sides laughing but managed to hold onto it and just smiled.

'Pardon?' he said.

'An apple and a banana!' said the second policeman impatiently, aware of how 'looking for a pair of 'fruits' may have sounded due to the ambiguity of the term 'fruit'.

Kenny looked through the doors of the pub and saw an apple and a banana scuttle out of the way at the sight of plod at the door. Kenny was still trying desperately not to laugh, though a chuckle was running round in his stomach trying to find its way out. Inside the bar John and Spit, two great characters in the city, loved by all and known as the infamous 'sway Twins' — because they always drank the Dip dry by about nine o'clock on a Saturday night and then spent the rest of the evening 'swaying' like trees in a storm — stood by the bar and watched dumbfounded as an apple and a banana dashed past them to the corner of the bar and ducked down to hide. They looked at each other as though to say 'fucking beer's on form tonight me fella me lad!'

'I don't know what you mean,' said Kenny trying to give Lee and Liam time to get out of the way.

The second PC, getting more impatient by the minute said,

'We've had a report that a banana assaulted a man in the city centre earlier this evening. Have you seen him?'

Kenny could hold himself no longer and burst out laughing. 'Have you two been drinking?' he asked, through his gleeful tears.

Unamused, the two policemen pushed past Kenny and entered the pub. At the sight of the law a group in the corner started chanting 'PLOD - PLOD - PLOD - PLOD - PLOD - PLOD - PLOD - PLOD!' As you can see we have a healthy respect for our police force in Coventry. By now Liam and Lee were well gone and only Cash was left, still dressed as a Lemon.

'Anything wrong, lads?' Cash asked.

The two PC's looked at each other, then back to Cash who was already starting to giggle.

'I don't suppose you've seen an apple and a banana have you? We've had a report that a banana . . .'

It was too much, Cash lost the plot and burst out into uncontrollable laughter. The officers left, embarrassed and with two dangerous pieces of fruit still on the loose.

'A' was a big man, bigger than a pie shop in fact, but could he move? He was one of the quickest men for his size that I have ever seen, and fit too. He was always taking money off people in bets because they couldn't believe that a man in excess of twenty-two stone could play squash. He used to destroy them on the court and then relieve them of their wager.

At the time when I was working the doors 'A' was the *Godfather* of Coventry doormen. He'd been in the job for about ten years then, and I was only just starting my apprenticeship. When he sent a message down to me at Buster's to say that he would like me to be on his team it was like being offered a part in Hollywood. After several years of working with him we became good friends and I was always impressed by his professionalism and absolute unequivocal cool. I stood with him one night when we were faced by three soldiers in the bar of the Pippin, all wankers who would give a decent soldier a bad name. One had pulled a knife, and all three were seconds away from 'entering the arena'.

'A', completely unperturbed by their aggression, psyched them out when he gently took a bottle of Pils out of the hand of the guy with the biggest mouth — it was a hard won contest to choose — like taking candy from a child, and slowly poured the contents over his head whilst telling him, very calmly, how annoyed they were starting to get him. It was the most humiliating thing I have ever witnessed and it was all I could do to stop myself from gagging with laughter. With beer all over his face and clothes he looked exactly like what he was — a fucking rectum.

'Now you had all better be going before I get any more annoyed.'

They all looked at him sheepishly, like children that had been caught in the cookie jar, and left with their reputations in tatters. They thought they were hard men but they were not even capable of spelling it. On another occasion this big man, hunting for a guy who had slapped his mother in a café, travelled all the way to London at three in the morning, after working all night on the door, to find his man. At 6 am he stood, stern faced and intent, knocking at the door of a rather large rastafarian. It was a bitter, wet morning somewhere in the south of the country's capital. Only the chink of distant milk bottles and the whistling of some other early birds could be heard.

The steel wrapped around 'A's' fingers felt cold to the touch and yet welcoming. 'A' didn't want to hurt his hands on this dirty bastard. The monster that answered the door was a big man in a scruffy string vest that sported stains down the front like he'd been in an egg throwing contest and lost. He was followed closely by a strong unpleasant smell so profound that it carried its own cartoon 'stink lines'. There were bits of old food hanging from his goaty beard and his eyes were only half open. He looked like shit. But then he was shit so that figures. He must have wondered how a man as big as 'A' had managed to fit into his eyeline all at once.

'Yea?' he asked, wondering if this was the new milkman and if so where the fuck was the milk?

BAAANG!! There was nothing to say really. Pain, as much as could be squeezed into as little time as possible, was the order of the day. A guy that hits your mum doesn't deserve words and anyway the last thing 'A' wanted was conversation with a scum bastard like this one. There was an explosion of splattering teeth from his mouth, like he was vomiting blood: it was a crimson and dental volcanoe. He reeled backwards, shocked beyond measure, the back of his head bounced off the door frame splitting his skull like a ripe melon. He tried to fall but 'A' didn't let him, it wasn't over yet, not by a long shot.

As he lurched forward 'A' grabbed him by the vest and smashed him again and again with the iron fist. The last punch sent him clean through his own front window and back into the house. 'A' followed him without demur and finished the job in the guy's own front room. When he had finished even his own mother wouldn't have recognised him.

It was a bloody affair. When the police arrested 'A' he said to their astonishment,

'Can you make it quick? I've got a golf game to attend.'

'A' was/is a keen golfer and good at that too. He used to practice on a local golf course in Bedworth which is a very little place just outside Coventry with a big head. Everyone in Bedworth seemed to think that they could 'have a fight', and whilst one or two could, the majority couldn't fight tiredness. Colin always said that being the best fighter in Bedworth was a bit like being the best fighter in your street, only there's probably more people in your street. Bedworth was small, you could probably carpet the whole place for fifty quid, I was gonna go there for a drink one night but it was shut, apparently it closes at ten. On another occasion I rang up the Bedworth football ground and asked, 'what time does the game start?' the guy at the other end of the line replied 'what time can you get here?'

Actually while I'm on the subject of Bedworth I must tell you about the night my friend Kev battered a whole football team. It was at a place I worked in Coventry called the Parrot, a lovely night club with a rep for a trouble free night, usually. Kev was a monster of a fighter with the best right hook this side of a John Wayne movie, but he was also a fair man. Along with Awesome Anderson Kev was one of the best leaders that I have ever had the pleasure of knowing. I first started working for him after my famous run in with the Bell Green crew (story in *Watch My Back*). Kev had also had a few run-ins with this crowd and despised them. When he heard about my encounter he offered me a job on his team. The club he ran had its own football team — mostly the players were from Bedworth — that they sponsored.

This particular night the team were in the club celebrating the fact that they had just won a trophy or something and they were acting up a little. We'd had our fair share of violence in the club prior to this and the management had told Kev that they wanted it curbed so he in turn said to us 'try not to hit anyone, just throw them out'. He was a fair man like that and although he had a high rep for fighting I never saw him hit anyone who didn't deserve it, in fact I remember him more for his humility than his fighting. I'd worked under him for a time and found his leadership to be unquestionable. The man was a walking legend. He had twelve men under him at the Parrot and every one a name fighter in his own right, a bit like the dirty dozen, and he had each and every one of us eating out of his hand. Not because he could have a fight nor simply because he was the head doorman, that didn't bring lasting respect. He got our respect because he was the most respectful man on the planet. For a man with several hundred fights under his belt — he was un-defeated — you might expect a monster with ignorance for an attitude. With Kev it was different. He was such a respectful person, a brilliant man manager that he had everyone wanting to do their best for him.

I remember watching him work one night; the guy was an inspiration and I learned many many invaluable lessons from him. They say that the best way to judge a man's character is to watch the way he treats someone who is not worth anything to him, someone who can give him nothing. A group of about ten young men were at the door to the club waiting to get in. At the back of the group stood a young man who looked slightly out of place, he was bit of a swot. The other lads hardly seemed to notice him almost as though they were ashamed that he was a part of their company. You know the sort, there is one in every work place, every night club, every classroom and every office. The guy that it's not cool to be seen talking to. That's exactly what this guy was and you couldn't help but feel sorry for him. He was thin and under confident, constantly trying to get in on the conversations but just as constantly getting knocked back. He was sadly lacking in kudos points, I doubt that he even knew what they were, probably thought Kudos was a new aftershave.

I thought it was only me that noticed these people and tried to make a fuss of them so that they feel more accepted. Apparently I was not on my own. Kev approached the group and everyone, all in awe of this great man, stood in anticipation. He by-passed all the leaders, all the popular lads in the bunch and went straight for the swot. He beckoned him on. The lad looked all around him, 'can't be talking to me' he must have thought.

'Yea, you,' Kev said. 'You're a good lad, you can come to the front of the queue.'

The other lads looked on and whispered to each other,

'I didn't know he knew Kev H!'

Almost as an after-thought Kev said to the lad, motioning to his friends,

'Are these lads with you?'

'Yea.'

'OK. They can come through, too. But they have to pay.'

The lad's face was a picture. He looked like he'd just won the lottery. I watched the group as they walked into the club, they were buzzing around this youth and excitedly firing questions at him. In the space of a minute Kev had turned this kid around, he was no longer the swot of the group, he was the one that knew Kev H and the bouncers at the Parrot. Kev hadn't noticed me watching and when he turned he seemed embarrassed that I had witnessed his deed.

'Ah, you know how it is, Geoff. I felt sorry for the lad. If they think that he knows me they'll treat him better.'

I smiled. It may seem a small thing to many but to me it was one of the most impressive displays of character I had ever witnessed. That's what made Kev a legend, not just the fact that he'd destroyed just about every 'heavy' in the city — I once watched him KO seven men in one night — it was his humility and innate kindness.

I digress, back to the football team: within minutes of his 'no violence' lecture the football team kicked off in the club, so, in we ran to get them out — without the use of brutality. Now this works OK when you are dealing with people who let you restrain them, but not too good when they start trying to hit you, as was the case on this occasion. One of the football team, we never did find out which one, made the grave mistake of punching Kev on the nose during the debacle. Kev's head went and he started hitting everything that moved.

When we finally managed to stop the team from fighting we lined them all up by the wall — like in an identity parade — and Kev walked along the line and 'dropped' every member of the football team, each in turn, until they all lay on the floor in a heap. It was his only way of knowing that he'd got the one who hit him, even if he didn't know which one it was. That was one match when they didn't collect the accolades.

So, we've established that Bedworth is a small place and small places like many small men (not wanting to sound 'small menist') often have a chip on their shoulder the size of Florida. This was certainly the case in Bedworth where it was hard even to drive through the town without getting into a fight with some lemon. 'A' was playing a round of golf with his mate on the Bedworth golf course, just getting a bit of practice in. As they came towards the third hole they noticed a group of five men sitting around the bunker drinking bottles of cider. They were drunk and loud and being abusive — just another day in Bedworth. 'A' tried to ignore them but was pretty bothered by the fact that these wankers were spoiling his golf and it was after all a private club. They had obviously broken onto the course because it was fenced off from the public. Still, he surmised, it was not really his problem and as long as they kept out of his world they'd be OK.

'A' was a cool guy but had a ferocious temper that was better not unleashed. I remember when he ran a pub in a notorious part of the city, ruled by an infamous crew. On his first day the crew, used to ruling the roost in this violent shit hole of an area, were all sat in his bar having a drink — probably about twenty of them. 'A' came from behind the bar and, to everyone's astonishment, he locked the front door to the pub. He actually locked them and himself in, and then walked into the middle of the crowd. What you have to bear in mind here is that these people had fucked just about every pub, pub landlord and doorman in the city at one time or another and as much as I despised them they were a force to be reckoned with. There were a few murmurs as the big man stood amongst them, and he said something like,

'This is my pub. I know who you all are, or who you think you are and I'm telling you now that if any of you ever fuck in my pub you'll have me to deal with. If you ain't happy about that then there is only one way out of this pub and that's on a stretcher. So if anyone's not happy let's do it now.' He eyed everyone of them who all looked at each other as though to say, 'hey, I'm happy about that, you happy about that?' 'Yea, no problem. I'm happy!' No takers. Not a pair of bollocks in the whole place. These guys may have been a force to be reckoned with as a gang, but, it would seem, on their own they were not worth a wank. It's easy to fight in a crowd because you almost become anonymous and you have the support system of other bodies. On your own your only support system is your own ability and the courage to go it alone. Not a one of these wankers had that and that's why I can't give them any respect. No doubt they won't be happy when they read this but hey, lads, you know where I am (and more importantly don't forget that I know where you are too).

Some months after this had happened, and still smarting from the embarrassment, they did chance their arm with 'A', about the same number again — there's a surprise. They stood outside 'A's' pub late one night shouting and screaming about what they were and were not going to do if 'A' didn't let them in. 'A's' head went and he fetched some sawn off hardware from the cupboard and pointed it at the boys. First they froze then one quipped,

'It's not loaded!'

BOOOOMMMMM!!!

'A' exploded one barrel in the air and then pointed the second at the boys who stumbled over each other in a bid to escape death. He had gone past the point of no return and was now actually trying to kill someone: BOOOOMMMM!!! He aimed it at three of the youths as they ran for cover and dived over a wall — just in time. In a millisecond the streets were as empty as a eunuch's pants and the courage of the infamous 'crew' was being trodden on like dog turd as they ran for their very lives.

'How come no one died?' I asked 'A' afterwards.

'Luck Geoff, pure luck,' he replied.

Back to the golf range. The five brain deads, surrounded by full and empty bottles of cider, were getting rowdier by the minute and shouting profanities at 'A' and his golfing buddy. They obviously didn't know what or who they were dealing with, otherwise they'd have had zips surgically placed over their big mouths to protect them from themselves, and save them the hiding they were going to get if they continued on their present course of action. Now call me perceptive but, given that 'A' is over twenty stone and was carrying a metal baseball bat, sometimes known as a golf club, you'd think these guys might have had an inkling that this was 'not the recommended course of action to be taking'. Not the wisest decision ever made and, for sure, not an intelligent man's bet. They surely should have known not to mess but no, they shouted and abused and laughed at every stroke 'A' and his friend swung. By their actions they forced an incident.

'A' still kept his cool and didn't say a thing. He understood drunks, he'd had a lifetime of them and knew that they probably didn't know what the fuck they were getting themselves into. But, a man's patience can only be stretched so far before it snaps. The final straw for 'A' came when he stood opposite the youths and tried to put his ball in the third hole. They wouldn't let him make his shot without hooting, and crowing and generally being abusive. 'A' had heard enough. He walked over to the bunker where they sat. He swung his club gently. From their viewpoint, sat on the ground and looking up through a cider bottle, he must have appeared to take up the whole sky line, as he got closer and bigger they probably thought it was a total eclipse of the sun. It very soon would be. He stood ominously over the 'cider five'. For a second they fell silent as though realising the error of their ways, then, without warning or cause the one closest laughed hysterically at 'A' and lifted a bottle of cider to his mouth.

CRAAASSHHH!!!

'A' swung the golf club with admirable accuracy and smashed the two litre bottle as it touched the drunk's lips. It exploded impressively in his face and drenched him, forcing a sharp intake of breath. The laughing ceased. CRASH!! CRASH!! CRASH!! CRASH!! CRASH!! In the space of a couple of seconds 'A' had smashed with his club every bottle of cider being held or on the ground. The Bedworth lads were open-mouthed with shock. You could bash their mothers and rape their sisters but never, ever smash their bottles of cider.

YAAHHHAA!!! As one they attacked 'A' ferociously from the bunker. It was a World War II all over again kind of scenario with punching, grabbing, kicking and gouging filling the screen. THWUUMP!!! THWUMP!!! 'A' managed to catch the first two with the full swing of his club and knock them for six, if you'll forgive the pun. An eye closed instantly on one, two teeth smashed and one tooth took a tumble from the mouth of another. It spiralled through the air looking lost and pathetic. For a second all eyes followed its descent until it landed and buried itself in the grass somewhere near the third hole. Blood covered their faces as 'A' hit everything that moved with the slice of his nine iron. There were too many for him and, because they had drunk so much the injured were getting back into the fight and, outweighing him like the skeleton soldiers in the fantasy classic 'Jason and the Argonauts'.

You can picture the scene: on the sleepy greens of a Sunday afternoon golf course, a huge black guy swatting five drunks with a golf club, two of whom were now swinging off his neck like winter scarves, one trying to hit him with bits of broken cider bottle, another on his hands and knees sifting through the grass looking for his broken teeth, the last breaking the minute mile in the opposite direction. 'A's' mate, admittedly not a fighting man, froze to the spot like a snowman in freeze frame. He just couldn't bring himself to help his friend. His bottle had well and truly gone and for years afterwards he would beat himself black and blue about it like so many people do. It happens, everyone has a limit.

THWAACK!! OHHH! A sickly blow from 'A's' iron struck and another of the 'cider five' lost a bodily part and bit the dust. At the sight of his mate splattered by the third hole another ran off, followed by one more. When the last one tried to run he was caught with a whack in the back of the head that tumbled him over pathetically in a slapstick somersault. A cartoon lump the size of a football rose on his head and he ran for dear life clutching his skull like his head might fall off. 'A' gave chase but for all he was worth his stamina had gone and he had to sit down to catch his breath. All the lads ended up in the casualty department of the local hospital and when they found out who 'A' was and that he was looking for them with something a little more potent than a nine iron they all contemplated emigration — perhaps suicide. It was only the skillful mediation of a middle man and enough expressions of regret to write a book on apologies that stopped 'A' seeking the ultimate revenge. Needless to say he never had trouble on a Sunday golf session after that day and his victims, the thick bastards, never, from that day to this, set foot again on a golf course. The moral of this little story? Don't fuck with twenty-two stone black guys bearing golf clubs.

7. The Cast

Let me give you an intro to some of the staff at Buster's night club: John was the main man — forgive me if you have heard some of this before — a person much admired by his fellow doormen. John was not a great man for sharing a smile or showing emotion, other than with his closest people. All his emotions, love, like, hate, joy were relayed tactiley or through the language of 'piss take', invariably, to those with translation difficulties, gross misinterpretation could, and often did, occur. One member of staff at Buster's once complained to the manager,

'John keeps putting me in headlocks and chokes.'

'Is that all?' said the relieved manager. 'That just means he likes you!'

It had obviously frightened the poor lad and we had to explain to him that this was John's way. The misinterpretation, though, was understandable because his way of telling you that he didn't like you was relayed in the same manner. To those of us who were close to and loved the man the difference was obvious. If he liked you, there was always the hint of wry smile as he placed you in a strangle that we liked to call 'the vice', or he simply took the piss out of you. If he was serious, his look was empty and cold and you usually found yourself unexpectedly unconscious.

John hardly ever spoke without the aid of sarcasm and he rarely opened his heart to anyone; he did to me at times but then I spent many hundreds of hours with him under some severe conditions. That brings you close to a person. He was absolutely devoted to his two young boys, and even with them his displays of fondness were via wrestling matches on the front room carpet where he would 'toughen them up so's they'd be ready'. Most people who met the man when he was working could not understand him or men of his ilk; they found him unapproachable and often intimidating.

I watched John many times with his boys and they loved him to death and found no such problem in interpreting dad's *special language*. They read every touch, look, nudge and push with a subliminal and innate sixth sense that all kids seem to possess. I loved John, I loved his way, but it must have been hard for women with men like John as they perhaps might not understand and appreciate the intricacies of hard men in a hard world. Whilst most girls got necklaces from their men appraising their fondness his lady might expect to get . . . a neck lock?! Whilst others are 'wowed' with flattering flirtations, she is given the intricacies of the carotid strangle or the one-punch knockout.

I have this problem too. I tell people that I like them by being physical. 'Gosh, he's knocked her clean out, he must really like her.'

Colin 'no neck' Maynard: I knew Colin long before his neck disappeared under a mass of deltoid and trapezious muscles; I knew him as a young thin lad, not unlike myself, who wanted to be BIG. We both believed that big was synonymous with tough. Now we have both 'danced the dance' we realise that big is a mental concept and not a physical one. The real bar bell curls that build mental muscle are not done on a physical level with bars and discs of steel, they are done on a mental level, confronting and handling adverse situations.

Training with the weights might give you physical size and strength — the obsession of many 'gym fighters' who even use steroids to attain their goal — but it means very little out there in the real world. Whilst the size and physical strength of these men increases, often the mental physique does not, and the man with the muscles never really becomes the mental powerhouse that he always associated with physical size. He becomes sixteen stone on the outside when really he had wanted to be sixteen stone within. This is a weakness that few see but certainly many big men perceive. They feel physically indomitable and yet at the same time they are a mental coward, though of course in reality they are not cowards, it is only their reasoning process mistaking natural apprehension for FEAR, a common fault with many people on and off the door. Sadly they find it difficult to share these feelings for fear that their peers might think them cowards, and so they live with misguided monsters in their minds that burgeon on ignorance. Being physically big they often feel more fear than most because the pedestal upon which they stand is higher, and often made of sugar. So they spend their lives balancing, very precariously, on an unsound foundation.

Anyway, back to Colin. He was a very moody doorman who put on a mask that said HARD. To me and the lads the mask was transparent and said nothing more than MASK, though it fooled most. Colin was a lovely bloke inside the shell of a tough guy. And he was tough when it was needed: he did some fucking brave things that used to astound me at times and when he let his guard down he could charm the birds from the trees. Col could move four hundred pounds on the bench press and must have weighed in at sixteen stone. For a big guy he could move a bit and had very fast hands. I have to repeat that being a good fighter is not the pre-requisite to being a good doorman, though it was an important factor on a hard door like this one. If there was a doorman on a team and he wasn't a great fighter his fighting capabilities would never be mentioned, as long as he was 'there' if the shit hit the fan. 'Being there' meant more than what you actually did 'once there'.

At once Colin could be cold and calculating and yet, paradoxically, almost childlike in his pranks, especially with the other doormen. In certain company and at certain times he could be playful though, as soon as he felt a threat or if anyone went for his title, he would slip the mask back on and become stand-offish and 'overkill cool'. He was rarely nice to women though this was again just the iron cloak he wore to veil his soft side.

On the door Colin was cold and unapproachable, at all times. We never found this a problem because me and Ricky more than evened the balance by making the ladies and gents feel 'special' and welcome. The hot and cold of the various doormen left the club with an over all feeling of 'warm'. Every doorman on the team — any team — has his good side and bad but they are all integral parts of the night club jigsaw. Some punters need the cold of Colin to keep them in place whilst others need the warm of me or Rick to keep them happy and make them feel welcome; others still need the sand blasting look of John to let them know not to 'fuck'. Over all, and this is only my own impression, Colin is a quiet, loving man enveloped by a 'hard cloak', those of us close to him could see through the façade.

Then there was Ricky, a beautiful person who was incredibly naive about life and about women — he thought that pubic hair was a mate of Bugs Bunny — and that was a part of the man's charm. Rick was hugely built at six four and seventeen stone and a native of Jamaica. He had spent the last ten years before Buster's as a pro boxer. He was always in high spirits and laughing hysterically in a high pitched giggle about something or other, and yet he spoke in very slow, slurred monotones, synonymous with his past as a pugilist of repute. Ricky had a heart of gold and was always very reluctant to revert to physical tactics though when he did it was usually always spectacular. Potential troublemakers often thought that because he spoke slowly he punched slowly too — they got a shock when he shot 'cripple shooting' punches that were usually felt before they were seen.

I loved Ricky and we spent many hours together on the front door at Buster's as 'searchers'. I searched the punters for weapons (if they didn't have any we didn't let them in for their own safety), Ricky watched my back. John didn't like Rick to search because if he had to turn people away for whatever reason, he took far to long to do it, going into the histrionics of 'why' they had been refused entry and 'why' the rules were as they were. Which is kind of nice but, in the meantime, other punters were becoming impatient waiting to get into the club. He was wonderful with the ladies, treating them very gently, and had a bit of a following among them, becoming almost baby-like in their company.

In actuality he was a walking paradox with a much scarred and broken face yet a persona that was so pure you felt you wanted to protect him. Not that he couldn't protect himself, of course: the man was number one contender for the British heavyweight title and once went eight rounds with the great John L Gardner. Even though Rick had many lady admirers he still kept it all very platonic. He was married at the time and very loyal to his wife who turned out to be not so loyal to him. He carried pictures of his children with him wherever he went and showed them off to anyone who would take the time. I saw the pictures so many times I started thinking they were my kids.

If a situation ever arose in the club Rick would always be right behind you 'watching your back'. As a back-up man he was second to none and if there was ever cause for him to hit someone he punched so hard that their ancestors felt it. Rick's problem, well it wasn't really a problem he was just a nice bloke, was that he was very reluctant to issue pain to others and that often placed him, inadvertently, in danger. John was always telling him off for this: doormen have died because of hesitation. Ricky always nodded when John dished the bollockings but never really changed, that was just his way I guess.

Rick also had a cheeky habit of suddenly disappearing at the end of the evening, always to be found on the dance floor gyrating to the sounds of the day with a lady admirer. John never liked this either because, as he would say, 'that's not what we're being paid for, if it kicks off and you're on the dance floor then you might as well not be here'. John was right of course, when you work the door the job description does not include 'dancing with the local talent'. It's hard to stay alert when you've got a beautiful pair of hips gyrating into your bits to the beat of *I'm Your Lady* by Jennifer Rush. I must admit I fell foul to this myself on the quiet nights, in fact for a while I used to get a dance every Tuesday night with the prettiest thing you ever saw who had a bottom to die for (that was always to Jennifer Rush too, I always asked for it especially). I still can't think about the girl without the blood rushing through my veins at a hundred miles an hour straight into my boxer shorts. If she entered the room I'd have to crawl out on all fives. The Tuesday night slow dance became a ritual and if she is out there, she's knows who she is, 'big kisses to you'. It's a sad story actually because I found out years later that this beautiful lady got addicted to heroin, lost all of her teeth as a consequence and became a wrinkled old lady at the age of only 28. I nearly cried when I heard, in some ways I wish I wasn't told, it really upset me. 'Radio Rental Rob' told me he had seen her in hospital and that she was 'on the way out'. I spent a year in the girl's arms on Buster's dance floor, and it upsets me no end to think about her in this way. To me she will always remain the beautiful young picture seller with the lovely bum.

The heroin thing was and is not uncommon, we had a receptionist, lets call her 'Needles', who went the same way. She was a tall, attractive 'rocker' type and the rudest girl in the western world. The way she treated some of the customers was fucking frightening, I'm sure she didn't know quite what she was doing sometimes. If the mood took her she would throw a customer's jacket on the floor when he went to take it off her and give looks that could kill an army. Mind you that wasn't as bad as putting raw sausages and half eaten food in their pockets, which is what Radio Rental Rob used to do as a hobby. How 'Needles' managed to hold down the job at Buster's was beyond everyone, mind you she was seeing one of the doormen for a while so that might have been an influence, though that shouldn't give anyone a licence to be a horrible bitch. She insulted the customers for no apparent reason and caused many fights in the club simply because we had to defend her from the angry punters who, rightly so, wanted to make her head into a canoe! As a paradox to this she could suddenly become an angel, as sweet as sugar, forcing even those who despised her to re-assess their feelings. Then, just as quickly she would turn nasty again. Her mood swings, we later found out, were due to heroin addiction. One of the doormen found her shooting-up in the ladies toilet one night. I have to say that I liked the girl and worked with her for a very long time without realising her problem, I just thought she was a bit psycho, but she was a sad case and when I later found out about the heroin a few of the weird things that she used to get up to fell into place a little. She was once a brilliant artist who had great prospects at Art College. Now, due to her 'need', she is destined to stay in grotty city centre night clubs helplessly hooked on a desperate habit.

When John gave Rick a bollocking — he was always having words with him — Rick apologised profusely for his dance floor antics and solemnly promised that it would stop, and it did . . . until some sweet thing with an eye for a smooch invited him onto the dance floor — then he carried on just the same as before. He was such a great guy that you just couldn't fall out with him over it. Colin was always winding Rick up about his reluctance to get into a fight. 'What do we have to do, Rick?' he would ask, 'ring a bell to start the first round?' As per usual Ricky would just laugh and start dancing around, he was definitely off the planet. He had a wonderful habit of misquoting clichés telling us in that slow, slurred yet gentle voice 'I'll count those bridges when I reach them,' or 'You've hit the nail on the button'.

Usually Ricky was the gentlest of men, but when he switched on he looked mean; the transformation was frightening. A good example of this reluctance to 'get it on' was the night he had a fight with a local Rastafarian. Rick had refused the guy entry to the club because he was wearing training shoes, they were against the dress code of the club. As is usually the case the guy argued the toss with Ricky who went into a long lecture about how he didn't necessarily agree with the rules but they were there and he had to enforce them. The Rasta, a huge aggressive looking man with long locks and a beard that made him look like Rasputin, suggested, rather unkindly an un-originally, that his refusal to the club was nothing to with the fact that he was wearing trainers rather it was because 'you're prejudiced!' The club, he said, held a colour bar. That's a good one. There was only one white guy on the door staff at the time and that was me so you could hardly accuse the club of enforcing a colour bar. There were quite a few people in the queue waiting to come into the club that night and there was a hum of anticipation as the two very large men argued it out. Some of the women moved away from what even they saw as an inevitable clash of titans.

For the record there was never any prejudice on this door, it was a ludicrous suggestion, though I have heard of unofficial colour bars in other clubs in the city. With us it was simply dress code: if the management said no pink socks we wouldn't let pink socks in no matter how pretty the legs that wore them. No trainers? Then the queen herself wouldn't get in with trainers on — not that she would come to Buster's night club on a Saturday wearing trainers of course (maybe on an alternative night, though).

This is one of the reasons why, when you have a code at a club, it has to apply to everyone, even your mates. If you have a ban on training shoes for instance then no one, and I mean no one, should be allowed past the door with them on. Even if the manager is on a night off and he visits the club he should not be allowed through the doors with training shoes. The worst thing in the world is when one of your best mates turns up for a night out and they are wearing jeans or trainers — really if they were good mates they wouldn't put you on the spot like that, but it happens. Picture the scene if you will. Your best mate turns up at the club, he's been out of town for a while and doesn't know that the club holds a 'no trainers' rule. He has a beautiful girl on his arm and he's brought her to the club to impress her because he knows the doormen and they'll make a fuss of him, let him to the front of the queue, let them in free, etc. What do you do? Do you make an exception to the rule just this once and let the man in or do you embarrass him by turning him away after he has already bragged to his date that he is 'best mates with the doorman'? What are you going to do? Use your discretion here, think it through. Should you let the man in — could you turn him away? I've had loads of old/ex mates say 'oh

that fucking Geoff, went up to see the man and he wouldn't
let me in because I had trainers on. What's that all about? He
used to be a great bloke — he's really changed since he started
doing the door'. Let's say for argument's sake that you let the
man in, just this once. What harm can it do? Once he's in the
club no one will know any how. It's pitch black in there. He's
in the club, having a great time with his lady, she's suitably
impressed that he's connected and everything is sweet. You're
at the door arguing with ten blokes from out of town about
the fact that they can't come into the club because they're
wearing training shoes. They're a bit heavy and not happy
about the verdict but you've insisted that it's nothing personal
and that no one gets into the club wearing trainers. They're
starting to calm a little and you think you've convinced them.
BOSH! Your mate and his lady leave the club — they fancy
an early night — smack bang in the middle of the argument.
What's the lad wearing? Training shoes that stand out like a
hard-on at a lesbian convention. I'll bet my house that you'll
be fighting with those ten blokes within seconds. Either your
rules apply to everyone or you don't bother having rules at
all. This incident is taken from experience, it happened to
me earlier on in my career and I learned my lesson well.

Understandably the racist slur upset Rick a little and an
argument ensued. Me, John and Colin watched as the
situation developed and couldn't help noticing that the Rasta
was starting to line Rick up by getting closer and turning
himself sideways on for a 'sucker' punch. He had also dropped
into single syllables which was another sure sign that he was
preparing to attack. When fight or flight is instigated blood is
drawn away from many of the non vital areas of the body,
that is those seen as non vital in fight or flight, and pumped
to those that are seen as vital. Subsequently a lot of blood is
drawn away from the brain, inhibiting speech, and that's why

many people struggle to speak when scared. At this point the novice street fighter often starts to drop into small sentences or single syllables like 'YEAH' 'SO' 'AND' etc. This tells the initiated that they're going to be 'having some' very soon. The perceptive, veteran street fighter would notice these signs immediately and take appropriate action — a pre-emptive attack or escape. Ricky didn't notice a fucking thing, he was so busy trying to convince the guy that he wasn't prejudiced that he didn't see the obvious.

Rick was old school — Queensbury rules, that kind of scenario — but he wasn't in the square ring now, on this patch there was no 'coming to scratch' and no touch of gloves before battle. This amphitheatre of violence is 'the pavement arena' where the latter, worthy prerequisites, are redundant and have been replaced by a congenital ritual of 'speak' and body talk. If you didn't know the language you were unlikely to win the battle.

'RICKY!!' I shouted as loud as I could and just in time. Ricky jumped back and just managed to weave under the thunderous right that would have eclipsed a horse. Rasputin had gone for it whilst he was being given the Bible according to Jabber James. A huge ring of people encircled the two men, myself and the lads moved off the step to blot out anyone who fancied backing the Rasta, we were watching Ricky's back.

The Rasta moved around Ricky, puffing out air and showing his fear as clear as if it were on a huge cinema screen. He threw some monstrous hand attacks that came by pigeon post, Ricky easily evaded them — but threw nothing back in return. As I said, this wasn't his arena: he was used the pomp and ceremony of the boxing ring where a bell signals the start and end of a round and a referee ensures fair play. In this arena there were no bells or flags, no start to the round other than the first punch thrown in anger and no end until one man was unconscious in a lake of his own blood. Up until now Ricky's size had gotten him out of most situations but this time his opponent didn't give a flying fuck, he was a big man himself, as big as Rick, and had sensed his naivety of things 'real'.

I looked at John and Colin for guidance: I didn't want to see Rick hurt because he was so nice. They shrugged their shoulders. I looked back at Rick who was exhausting 'running' space at a rate of knots. I knew that if he didn't strike back soon he would be on the floor with 210lbs of Rasta crawling all over him like an army of ants. Any minute now it was going to happen, I could tell.

'RICKY! JAB! JAB! COME ON, JAB!' I shouted as loud as I could, like a good corner man. Miraculously, Rick listened to my instructions and lashed out a jab that sent the Rasta into 'hyperspace'; he flew backwards like he'd been shot. His face flapped open like sliced sirloin and Rick moved towards him for the kill — but didn't take advantage. I shouted again:

'RICK! JAB CROSS, JAB CROSS!'

BA-BANG!! He threw a jab cross to order and, even though he only hit the guy in the chest ('he was to easy to hurt that's why I hit him to the body,' Rick said to me later) he still knocked him down two flights of concrete stairs behind him. His head thumped off every step as he fell — Rick's aim was good — and he tumbled to the bottom like a bad stunt man in a cheap movie. He lay at the bottom like a like a pile of blooded rags.

As is usual, it's almost expected, Rick received the perfunctory death threats and was informed that the Rasta was going to chop him up with a machete. Nothing ever came of it and, after a couple of weeks, it fell into the annals as 'just another fight'. This is something that I always try to remember when aftermath bites and the threats of 'comeback' come thicker than red letters through the door. 99% of them never materialise. Talk is cheap and everyone who takes a battering usually soothes his ego and defends his pride by telling his mates that 'this isn't over by a long shot'. But it's just hot air.

That's not to say that you do not take precautions, you have to just in case. Whenever I've dealt with a name fighter I always 'carry' for a month afterwards, just in case I get the 'team visit'. I make sure that I'm ready and my personal security is on red alert. Even at home every room, even the toilet, is equipped with an equaliser that is quick to hand so that, should I be attacked, I can reach something that will make multiple attackers more manageable. What I also do, as a matter of course, is get the home address of anyone who starts to make threats, then I let them know via the grapevine — or I might even phone them up if I feel it needs it — that I have their address and that the minute my address is visited, theirs will be also. It works. Most people who get personal don't like it when you want to get personal too.

I know what some of you out there are thinking, you're thinking 'a weapon in every room of the house, that's a bit paranoid isn't it?' Let me tell you that no matter where I am in the house I have an implement that can and will maim or kill anyone that thinks about stepping into my world, and I'll do it without blinking an eye. Turning up at a man's house is the ultimate insult, the worst thing you can do unless you are really prepared to kill or die for it. When you go to a man's home — I have only done it three times when the situation demanded — you force him not only to fight for himself but for his family too. An Englishman's home is his castle, as they say, so fucking well keep away unless you want your head made into a canoe or you are really serious about what you are doing. So before you go 'a visitin' ask yourself one thing, because it is very likely to happen, 'how are you going to feel when they do a return visit to you?' It's hard, but the fact is when you work the door this type of madness is the norm.

You also have to look at the legal aspect if you want to stay out of jail for any length of time. Entering someone's home and attacking them can get you sent to jail, without passing go or collecting £200, for a very long time. So if you do it, it'll need careful planning and a dozen witnesses who are prepared to stand up in a court of law and say 'he was with me all night M'lurd'. One of my ex students once said to me, 'Geoff, I'm thinking of working the door, what do you think?' Hard question, and not one that I could answer. Working the doors is a very personal thing and there is a lot at risk: your life, your liberty, your health, your family, sometimes even your sanity. I know one guy in the city who went off his trolley due to over exposure to violence, I know a few that have ruined their potential careers as pro boxers because they were seduced by the door, I know of half a dozen who spend one day a week in the psychiatrist's chair because they can't look at anyone, even people they know and love without lining them up for a right cross or a headbutt — that's what over exposure to violence does and if you don't understand what is happening to you, you could quite easily lose the plot.

I tried to explain this to Alan, a producer friend of mine, and he thought it rather barbaric, but he probably did exactly the same with his own job. I bet that Alan can't sit down and watch a play on the TV at night without throwing a critique on the lighting, the acting, the direction etc, because that's his job. He can no longer fully enjoy a TV (Television not Transvestite) programme like you and I because making these programmes is his living, so he can't help being an armchair critic. The bricklayer finds it hard not to look at the brickwork of everything around him, he can't walk down the street without looking at brick walls and checking the perps, the levels, the jointing, the standard of brick, the workmanship because that's what he does eight hours a day six days a week all of his life.

As a doorman you're no different except that your job is people, in particular violent people, and you have to learn if and when they are going to 'kick it off' and pre-empt them before they do. If you think that they're going to 'go' then you have to prime them like a painter primes a sill so that when you go for the 'gloss' you get a polished job. You have to know people like a 'trowel' knows brickwork and a producer knows the theatre. You have to learn to read bad intent at a hundred yards and be able to know who and what constitutes a threat so that you are the hammer and not the anvil. And looking for bad intent in others has a negative effect on the rest of your life because you can't just switch it on and off like a a tap, it becomes a part of you. This has an overflow into your every day life, of course it does, it has to, that's what you do every night of the week. So in your every day life you size people up — 'What if he starts?'; 'He's open to a right hand'; 'His chin looks a bit suspect'; 'Fuck me, what about that guy, he's a monster. I'll play it down and pretend that I don't want to know then hit him so hard with a right hook that his brain thinks it's a cabbage'. Does that make sense? Violence climbs inside your head and eats you away so that, unless you catch it in time, everything you think about starts to revolve around ways of damaging people who step into your world. This is OK when you're dealing with some fucking lowlife from Bell Green who wants to 'dance' but it's complete overkill when you're having an argument with the next door neighbour because his music is a little loud. This man does not need eclipsing, a physical response is hardly necessary — the guy's a fucking bank manager, his idea of confrontation is not a 'toe-to-toe' on the car park, it's a lively debate across the boardroom table. Doing the door is not your job, it's your life.

So, anyway, I asked my ex student 'how do you feel about the 2 am phone call that says 'we're gonna kill your wife and kids?'' He went pale, 'I wouldn't like that!'. 'Well mate, don't do the door then, because although that may never happen to you, it could happen on your very first night. It's certainly happened to me.' He didn't do the door.

Taking precautions is, for me, a lesson learned. One of my friends — an excellent doorman and a guy that can really handle himself — had a run-in with a heavy family in the city and was threatened with 'comebacks'. He, like the rest of us, had heard that story before, so was not over impressed with it; he certainly didn't expect a home visit. For his lack of preparation he paid dearly when the three brothers he had upset paid him a 'home visit' one quiet Sunday afternoon. I mean, who would expect it? Sunday afternoon after a few pints at the local, sitting down dozing in front of the TV, when: CRASH!!! CRASH!!! CRASH!!! The front door was kicked down and he was suddenly yanked from his stupor by six arms and dragged to the floor. Within seconds he was already semi-conscious on his back with six feet stamping all over his head. These guys were not trying to give him a slap they were trying to kill him. The beating was ferocious and bloody. One of the men dragged my friend's wife by the hair and locked her out of the room (she was four months pregnant at the time), and on his way back he grabbed a heavy cast iron saucepan and an iron from the kitchen. Whilst the other two held him down he smashed all his fingers until the bones snapped and protruded through the skin. The room was awash with blood and the involuntary grunts of pain as he came in and out of consciousness. His wife could be heard screaming helplessly in the other room. The pan and the iron were then used as bludgeoning tools all over his body, his face was smashed beyond recognition — he looked like elephant man — and every joint on his body was savagely attacked until it swelled to twice its normal size.

Songs of praise played on the TV in the background, unaffected by the heinous beating being enacted. Everything became a sleepy haze. He was still only half awake and couldn't think straight. He had no time to collect any kind of rationale for the attack. As he tried to bring some kind of logic to the fore, the saucepan struck him once again across the face. It landed with a nauseating, slapping thud, an arrow of pain shot through his head. His instinct was to try and jump up and get into in a better defensive position. This thought was stopped in its tracks by another strike with the iron across both eyes. The pain racked his whole body and before he could react it struck again and again and again. The attack from the three men was savage and frenzied. His eyes closed with the swelling.

Through the strikes, kicks and punches he could just distinguish the flailing forms of the 3 men and hear the hysterical screams of his wife in the background. They seemed totally intent on beating him to death. He managed to turn away and wrap his hands protectively over his face, but not before his cheek bone cracked with the next impact. He raised his hands again for protection and his fingers took the full force of the following blows, the bones turning to dust with the impact. He felt sick with pain. As he pulled his throbbing hands out of the line of fire his nose and lips burst open as the pan whipped across my face yet again. He could hear his attackers panting with the effort. His hands immediately and instinctively came back to his face only to take another blow across his broken fingers. The next shot hit him across the pubic bone and he curled up in a writhing ball of agony. He must have prayed that the beating would stop. Unfortunately it didn't and the next blow knocked him unconscious.

When he came to he was being dragged, sack-like, across the floor by his arms, being kicked, punched, spat on and shouted at en route. He was dumped, swollen and bleeding by the kitchen door. He desperately tried to move, to protect himself but was locked in a spasm of excruciating pain. It spread through his whole body. He felt like a bomb had gone off in his head and his faced throbbed with pain. Again he fell in and out of consciousness, his eyes were now completely closed with the swelling. Hoofing kicks in the head knocked him out and toe kicks to the body brought him back around again.

'GET ME A KNIFE! GET ME A KNIFE! I'M GONNA CUT HIS ARSE!' one of the men shouted. Foam spluttered from his lips. He looked like a rabid dog. The saucepan man raced back into the kitchen and frantically fumbled through the draws for a knife — they were going to stick it up his rectum and slit his arse all the way down to his balls and all the way up to his spine with the serrated edge. This they knew would take a fucking lot of healing and would be remembered for a very long time.

The word 'knife' brought him back to consciousness before his mind could fully prepare. He tried to open his eyes once and sharp stabs of pain raced through his eyeballs and into his brain. He closed them again to ease the hurt. Rivulets of blood pooled around his head. His smashed fingers twitched involuntarily. The two men continued to kick him in the face, body and genitals and anywhere else they felt it was suitable to kick and punch him. Their shoes and trouser turn-ups were soaked in my friend's blood. His body didn't know where to hurt first, or indeed most. The hysterical verbal abuse that had run parallel with the beating became indefinable as his swelling ears took kick after kick. All the words mushed into a distant screech. He felt like he was dying. He was.

Back in the kitchen the saucepan man yanked at the knife draw but it collapsed and fell through into the sealed cupboard below: as hard as he tried he just couldn't reach a knife. My friend had been meaning to fix the broken drawer for several weeks and his wife had been getting onto him to 'get it fixed'. In retrospect he was glad that he had forgotten otherwise, well, who knows?

The beating must have lasted about twenty minutes. The men eventually ran off and an ambulance was on the spot very quickly afterwards. My friend died in the ambulance, three times, and was resuscitated three times. When they got him to the hospital he was sent straight to intensive care where he spent the next month doing a very good impression of 'Michelin man'. On the stretcher on the way to intensive care he came to from one of his many blackouts, lifted his smashed hands and looked long and hard at his fingers: they looked like anything other than fingers and were smashed beyond recognition. Before he passed out again he asked the nurse,

'When I'm healed will I be able to play the piano?'

She smiled,

'Yes, I think so.'

'That's funny, I couldn't play it before.' He passed out. Counting the court case (the attackers only got two years!), which I can't go into, my friend had to live with this hanging over him for over a year. When I spoke to him at the time he said that he wished he'd have had a weapon to hand when they broke down the door, then he might have had a chance. Kind of makes you think, doesn't it? So in the aftermath watch your back and tool up — just in case.

Taking the piss, laughing in the face of danger, is a safety mechanism that most doormen develop and use innately. Recently I went with a friend of mine, Ian, to 'see' a guy that was heavy in the city and needed a talking-to. Ian had battered him once already and wanted to 'visit' with the lad just to make sure that it was well and truly over. On the way to the meet someone warned us that the guy, a local drug dealer, was carrying a gun so we should be on our guard.

Now, when someone tells you this kind of thing you can't help but feel extreme fear, but you know that you have to go see him anyway so this fear has to be over ridden. One of the techniques that you instinctively develop on the door, or in any physically dangerous job or endeavour, is to laugh in the face of danger. In this case I looked at the guy giving us the gossip and then at Ian and laughed. I pointed at my Rolex Submariner and said,

'Who wants the timepiece if I catch a bullet? Oh, and tell Sharon that I said I love her.'

Everyone laughed and the gun talk was forgotten. We did deal with this person and he wasn't carrying a gun. You have to remember, too, that just because the local gossip says the guy's got a gun doesn't mean jack shit, he just wants to gossip and see you sweat. As I have said in my other books gossips can be dangerous because they spread panic, which is highly contagious if you let it off the leash. As a leader, a head doorman or an experienced doorman it's your job to keep a check on the individuals that spread the 'bad news', to get rid of them and/or expose them for what they are — fucking idle gossips that make a long night for anyone with sensitive ears.

I remember the night I was working a door where there had been some serious trouble with heavy threats of 'comeback' from a notorious quarter of the city. I had been brought in to 'beef up the door' as it were until the threats subsided. Everyone was a little anxious because of the threats and because the people involved were notorious for revenge attacks. I stood in the reception area of the club this particular night and noticed that the other doormen, about five in all, were huddled in the corner listening to a story teller. I got closer and lent an ear.

'So,' I heard him tell the spellbound doormen, 'that's what I heard. They're getting guns and this thing is going to get bloody. I just thought I owed it to you to tell you the score. You just don't know how heavy these people are.' He continued talking in the same vein for several minutes and I could see the doormen getting more and more worked up, the circle got tighter and tighter and the story teller was in his element.

I had heard enough. This guy was climbing inside my people and tearing them up. I had to do something but I didn't want to over react, that would just add weight to his stories. I walked up close to them and the story teller looked at me and then back to his audience awaiting his next story with baited breath.

'What's that smell?' I asked. The lads all looked up from their circle. 'Oh, I know what it is,' I said when I had their attention, 'it's just the smell of bullshit!'

For a second there was silence until the penny dropped. As one all of the lads cracked up laughing and started shouting at the story teller,

'Yea, bullshit. You're full of bullshit.'

'It's only what I heard,' he said pathetically, his spell broken. For the rest of the night the lads tore into the story teller and ridiculed everything he said until he had to leave the club to escape the barracking.

The king piss taker of all time had to be Kenny the body builder. Kenny was everyone's friend, all the time. He never fell out with anyone. No matter whether you saw him first thing in the morning or last thing at night, at a funeral or at a wedding, the lad was happy and wearing an ear to ear smile emblazoned across his pale face like a party joker. Seemingly a confirmed bachelor though only still in his early thirties Kenny was always surrounded by women but never with a women per se. He is a very choosy man.

In ten years of knowing this personable guy — someone I class as a good friend — I have only ever known him date a handful of women and they were all beautiful. Tony B was always winding him up saying that he was a 'shirt lifter', a closet gay or a 'shit stabber'. Kenny just laughed it all off and said he wasn't and that he only helped them out when they're busy. He's only small in height for a doorman at five four though with tremendous strength and physique.

As doormen go you have talkers who can 'talk the talk' and walkers who can 'walk the walk'. 90% of the time the talker is excellent using guile as opposed to force to handle a situation, during the 10% that calls for a bit of 'physical' the talker is about as much use as a one legged man in an arse kicking contest. Paradoxically the 'walker' is worth his weight in gold during the latter 10% (physical) but as welcome as syphilis during the former 90% (talking). Ideally a doorman should be able to 'talk the talk' and 'walk the walk', but this takes intelligence. Kenny's a rare breed that falls into both categories: he is brave enough to confront situations and has the ability to 'hurt' when pain is the necessary antidote, and he can talk a situation down if verbal is the order of the day. Every doorman in any given team has a role to play, perhaps like an army unit that needs a pilot, a radio expert, an ops man, someone on the front line who likes the feel of steel and even a man at the back to 'clean up the mess' after it is all done; not everyone is equipped for the 'killing room'. Kenny could have a fight but in all the years I worked with the man I never once saw him hit another person, he was so good at talking people down that he rarely, if ever, had to become physical. That's why, in this city, he's a 'name' doorman — even though he doesn't bust heads every night of the week — who can and has filled every position, this is the type of doorman who knows when and how to talk, when to fight and when to run like fuck.

Then there's Winston. Me and this man were like brothers. He was singularly the best puncher I have ever had the privilege of working with. We've shared some heavy moments together, I guess that's why we're close, a couple of which I cannot, for legal reasons and reasons of confidentiality, share with you in this book. Needless to say I think the world of him. Gamacian born, Winston was a pro middle weight boxer with a sure fire chance of a title until he smashed his hand irreparably in the boxing ring and retired the square ring for a place at the infamous Buster's door. I used to stand in awe of this man when he lent his hands to work and spent many many hours in his tuition trying to get my own technique closer to the standard of his.

Ironically all Winston ever wanted to do was kick. He was fascinated by the kicking arts and I gladly swapped my knowledge for his. I watched him on more occasions than I can remember absolutely eclipsing wrongdoers; even in the midst of a dozen flailing bodies he would and could bob and weave and then let the most awesome of punches go. When he made connection bodies dropped like they'd been shot.

One night, though, his hands got him into a little trouble with that demon of discord 'aftermath'. The scenario was a familiar one, the same kind of stuff that usually starts a fight at a night club door, refusing people entrance. Winston and

D had stopped some men at the door because one of them was wearing tracksuit bottoms. The usual argument ensued:

'Why won't you let us in?'

'Because you're wearing a tracksuit.'

'No. It's not that. You just don't like us.'

'It's nothing personal, we just don't allow tracksuits into the club.'

'Yea, sure you black bastards!'

Same old scenario, you know the story. This went on for maybe twenty minutes and in the end, after much heated debate, the disgruntled punters wandered away from the club leaving a trail of racist profanities in their wake. Winnie and D were well pleased to have sorted the situation without any violence, the guys looked handy and it might have been a war. Unfortunately, an hour later they returned. By now Winston and D had found out who the men were, they were name fighters from one of the rougher parts of the city with a high rep for things violent. The chap who had been wearing a tracksuit was now wearing trousers, apparently his mate had gone home and they had swapped bottoms. He thought that this might have made a difference. It might have if his parting statement had not included 'fucking niggers', and one or two other choice words that left a bad taste in the mouth of D and Winston.

'I've changed my trousers. Can we come in now?' he asked. The four hard looking men, in their mid twenties, stood at front of the door. Winston looked them over.

'Naw man. You can't come in here.' Winston's broad shoulders blocked the entrance way to the club, D stood just behind watching his back.

'What's the fucking problem now? I got trousers on.'

'Doesn't matter. You're the problem, not your trousers. Your attitude is bad. Change your attitude, not your trousers.'

All four moved forward menacingly. Two were well known boxers of repute who could really 'have a fight', the others well known street fighters. The air was tense. The move forward, closing the distance, was a countdown to attack. Winston put up his fence, his lead left hand, and blocked the distance with a stop sign.

'You're not coming in so stay away from the door.'

The 'tracksuit' edged closer, hiding his distance close down with practised verbal.

'Wot's up with ya? We ain't gonna cause no grief. We just want a late drink.'

D piped up from the back,

'You're wasting your time, lads. You're not going to get in the club tonight.'

'Who the fuck asked you?' It was 'tracksuit' again. He stepped forward and his chest touched Winston's fence. Winston pushed him back. The fence is an early warning system that enables the user to read bad intention. If they touch the fence once then they're potential trouble, if they touch it twice they are definite trouble. Never let anyone touch the fence twice if you like your face the way it is. Tracksuit touched the fence again.

BANG!! Winston hit him with a mighty right that separated 'tracksuit' and his front teeth quicker than a speed dentist. He flew backwards and Winston closed the door.

Winnie and D stood inside the club and watched the three men (on the CCTV screen in the small cloakroom) looking around the floor for the decapitated tooth. When it was found, and with no further ado, they wandered off. The lads were surprised that they had gone without a fight, pleasantly surprised I have to say. They couldn't believe that these men, all name fighters, had gone without at least kicking the doors a couple of times, it didn't add up. They felt pretty sure that there would be some comeback before the end of the night. Every time the door knocked for the rest of the shift they expected trouble, a team of attacking animals baying for blood.

It never happened. They didn't show. At the end of the night the lads, both relieved that they'd had no recall on the incident, sat down and had a staff drink before making their way home. Winston left first and D came to the door just to make sure that there wasn't a team waiting to enact their revenge. Neither man nor beast anywhere to be seen. D went back in the club and Win climbed the concrete stairs to the car park that the night club was built under.

It had been an exhausting night. Anticipation seems to take up more energy than actual confrontation. Most of the lads I worked with over the years agreed, they'd much rather have ten fights in one night than wait for one fight all night, it makes for a very long shift. Anticipation also uses up masses of energy, that's why you get so tired when you're stressed. Even though the brain only weighs 2% of the body weight it can, in times of stress and anticipation, use upto 50% of your oxygen. That's why chess players often loose 7lb in weight over a week of tournament even though they eat the same as they usually do. This is also one of the reasons why people lose weight in times of worry.

It was three in the morning and dark. The moon shone down on the huge rooftop car park like a heavenly floodlight. Cold air smoked from Winston's mouth like he'd swallowed a dry ice machine. He walked steadily towards his BMW. The world was asleep. It's a great feeling at that time of the morning because it's as though the whole world is your own back garden — you own the whole lot. The only sounds on the whole globe were that of his own footsteps as they echoed a beat on the tarmac below him, and the ringing in his ears from five hours of constant, loud music. His head was already sharing the warmth of a bed with his lady in nearby Rugby where she awaited him like a coal fire on a winter's night. Only tonight he wasn't going to make it home — he had a date with destiny.

Out of a shadowy corner of the deserted car park two men emerged menacingly like night demons, one carrying a 5 ft solid tarmac pole that must have weighed 30lbs. Winston was oblivious to his fate, he was too busy searching his pockets for the keys to his BMW. He failed to notice them as they approached from his back, wielding their killing tool like an executioner's axe. They were experts and had walked this seedy path more times than most walk to the newsagent on a Sunday morning for a copy of *The Sport*. It's hard not to switch off at the end of the night, even though you know you shouldn't. This is often the most dangerous time for a doorman, when you think that the danger is over. You're three feet from the safety of your car, ten minutes from the safety of your home, half an hour from the sanctuary of sleep and for the sake of a few more minutes of awareness you pay the price.

I never switch off, whether I'm going for a piss in a public toilet or sitting in a city restaurant I position myself, in a cubicle or at a corner table, with my back to the wall and facing the door, so that I am ready for battle. Many people switch off their zanshin-awareness prematurely, and it often costs them their lives. In days of old Ninja, assassins would wait in the cess pit underneath a Samurai's toilet and sit in wait for their 'mark' to use the toilet: this they knew was when most men lose their awareness. They'd wait until the Samurai was half way through doing his business then ram a spear up his rectum and through to his stomach, killing him decisively. That's definitely what you would call foul play.

Unaware of Winnie's fate, the rest of the staff left the club via a different exit to be taken home by the club taxi driver

'The Archbucket of Cunterbury' as 'Radio Rental' had nick named him. Every night club has its own taxi driver that takes the staff home at the end of the night; Buster's was no different. This man, though, was a fucking menace, and always reminded me of a serial killer just waiting to happen. His cab was a shrine. Not a spec of dust in sight. He was one of those annoying types that had never had a crash in his life — don't you just hate that — and never, ever broke the law whilst driving. If the limit was 30 miles an hour then that's what the man did, and didn't he like to tell everyone about it. He was a tall, spindly man who looked like a fucking ghoul on loan from a Hammer Horror movie, he always reminded me of one of those de-frocked vicars you read about in *News of the World* with three wives and half a dozen love-children. The way he used to ogle at the young bar staff put you in mind of a white-macked flasher. The end of the night was always a nightmare for the girls he dropped off because he'd set his route so that the prettiest of the bunch was left alone with him until last. He thought the girls fancied him because they would creep around him flatteringly so that he'd drop them off first, or at the very least not last! Rumours about him being a, behind the bushes, 'park-poser' were rife. Rob reckoned he'd been 'done' for receiving 'swollen goods'.

WHACK!! Winston took the full force of the heavy bar across the back of his legs and his ankle snapped like a twig. He let out an involuntary cry of pain as he fell heavily by the side of his car and tried instinctively to crawl underneath to protect himself from the following blows.

'Fucking nigger,' one shouted through puffs of exertion as he wailed the heavy bar into the legs and body of Winston yet again. His cries of pain could be heard by no one, the town was empty, the car park desolate, he might as well have been in the middle of the desert. He felt sure that these men were going to kill him. D ambled from the club and climbed the concrete stair to the car park. He could hear muffled cries for help and what sounded like someone hitting a tree with an axe. It wasn't until he got to the top of the steps that he recognised the voice shouting in pain — it was Winston's voice, and two others shouting profanities.

He ran to Winnie's aid and saw two men standing over him, kicking and striking with a large bar. They'd noticed D as well and smiled when he ran straight past them. 'Lost his bottle,' they must have thought. D broke the minute mile to get to his car some hundred yards further down the car park. He quickly opened the boot. There it was, lying neatly by the back, wrapped in cloth like a piece of art — the equaliser. Three and a half feet of shiny, stainless steel baseball bat kept in the car for just such occasions. He whipped it out of the boot and unwrapped the cloth, he held it firmly in both hands and lifted it in the air like a sacred word. It felt light in his hands but he knew from the practice he had put in on the heavy punch bag that this baby could do the business in the hands of expertise. He turned quickly at the sound of running feet, the guy with the tarmac pole was running towards him with the bar above his head. D stood his ground and waited for the inevitable attack. He recognised the man as one of the group they had turned away earlier in the night. It was a long three seconds and he overrode the natural instinct to run for his life. Part of his strength lay in that he knew how to use the weapon in his hands, it felt as familiar as a spanner to a mechanic. He'd also been at this doorway many times before and knew the arena.

The 'pole man' stopped as he reached D and for a second that seemed to last a lifetime they looked into each other's eyes. 'Pole man' moved around D like a prize fighter looking for an opening, rocking the pole in both hands as though building momentum for the attack that was inevitable. He sucked in air like there as a shortage; this told D that he was unfit and probably only had a few seconds of fight in him. His nostrils flared like a wild bull and his breathing quickened. He was preparing to attack. D stood firm, controlled his breathing and focused every ounce of his being onto the man in front of him. One wrong move, he knew, meant at worst death, or at least irreparable damage. He held the bat light and firm, right hand on the handle, left had gently cradling the head. This gave him the option of both attack and defence. His whole body was now vibrating with adrenalin, so much so that it almost hurt. He smiled. 'Pole man's' upper lip rode involuntarily over his teeth and he snarled like a dog ready to bite, then lunged forward.

WHOOSSH!! He swung the bar so hard that it cut a sound as the air rushed out of its way: it was aiming straight for D's head. He thrust his steel bat hard into the air, one hand at either end to meet the bar and block its path. He felt the vibrations of metal hitting metal like a bodily earth quake. The connection was so violent that the bar flew out of the hands of 'pole man' and he lurched forward to his own right. D quickly changed his grip for the conventional head hitting hold and whipped the bat quickly and precisely, with seventeen stone behind the swipe, down onto his assailant's head. He recalled afterwards that it was almost like a beheading.

BANGGG!!! The strike echoed all around the car park. 'Poleman' fell pathetically to the ground, head first. His chin hit the tarmac and his face scraped along the floor, opening an ugly contusion the length of his face and taking off the front of his nose.

BANG! BANG! BANG! D ran up and down 'pole man's' body with the bat and gave the unconscious — already in a coma — man a bit of what he had given Winston. He left the youth for dead and then ran for his oppo who was still beasting Winston. At the sight of this huge black guy with a bat that shone in the night sky like a *Star Wars* 'light sabre' he ran for his very life. Who could blame him?

'Poleman's' blood covered a large area of the car park; even from where D stood some hundred yards away he could see the rapidly expanding lake of crimson glistening in the moonlight and hear the sickly gurgling as 'pole man' swallowed his own life force. Winston was in a pretty bad way, too. D had to carry him back to the night club where an ambulance was called. He left 'pole man' to fate. He was in a much worse state than Winnie, he was drowning in a pool of his own blood and deeply comatose. As soon as the ambulance took him to hospital he was placed on a life support machine and the critical list. Later, when the police told D that they thought he was going to die he replied, 'Good, the sooner the better.' He meant it. That was D.

Winston was off work with his injuries for a couple of months and 'pole man' eventually woke up with a headache that would last for a lifetime. He had been in a coma for several weeks. Incredibly, no one was convicted by the police and though threats of reprisal were sent from the opposition to the club none ever came. I guess that it was even, they got Winston, D got 'pole man' — an eye for an eye.

Radio Rental Rob was one of my favourite characters on the Buster's door. He is a good friend to this day and still works the doors in the city after twenty years. He also works by day as a security man in one of the big shopping centres in the city centre. When I started the door as a young, naive twenty-four year old karate black belt Rob was already a recognised veteran with more scalps to his name than Geronimo. He proved to be one of my greatest influences, one of the people who helped guide me through the labyrinthian trade we call 'Bouncing'. To me, Rob was everything that a good doorman should be: polite, respectful, helpful and courteous, though he was a bit of a scamp and loved to 'play the field' a bit — which got him into a lot of trouble when he worked at Buster's.

Rob was a master of 'talking the talk' but when it 'kicked off' he could change into a raging demon, it was almost a metamorphosis. Hence the nickname 'Radio Rental' (mental). It was rare that I ever saw him 'go' because he was so good at talking, that's one of the reasons I liked him so much. A more humorous and colourful character you couldn't wish to meet. He was a talented leader of people and, to my mind, wasted on the door, but as the man himself says 'it pays the rent'.

Those who have read *Watch my Back* will remember Rob from the 'blow job' incident in Buster's that I wrote so affectionately about.

Rob also had an uncanny way of seeing celebrity likeness in other people that you wouldn't notice until he pointed it out. He also had his own little names for people, for instance the taxi driver I spoke of earlier. Rob loved winding the man up, said he looked like a cross between Dr Death and an archbishop. He was tall and bowed with his shaky hands and 'sawn off' trousers — he looked like a crypt kicker. Rob called all gay men 'moses' — there were a fair few on the staff at Buster's — and would accuse them in a Sergeantly tone of 'receiving swollen goods'. The lesbians were simply referred to as 'strap-ons' or 'shotput catchers'.

One night one of the managers, who was a 'moses' by the way, asked Rob to assist him down the cellars with a barrel. Rob eyed him up suspiciously and said 'as long as I can remain in the vertical position, and not be forced to receive swollen goods'.

Being a Leo Rob was, as he will readily tell you, a natural eccentric who was always up to mischief. His deeper side, though, was a sensitive, deep thinking man with a love of people. I love the guy. His background is full of sadness with broken relationships littering his life path. The worst part about this, apart from losing and hurting some beautiful women, and of course being hurt himself, was losing his daughter Lisa to his first relationship. She was a big blue eyed baby girl with fair hair and an angelic smile that could melt a polar ice cap. She was the apple of Rob's eye. She's twelve years old now but Rob hasn't seen her since she was two.

As a young doorman he had a reputation for fighting and more than once paid for it — at Her Majesty's pleasure. Once, after taking on a whole crew singlehandedly at a Leamington night club he ended up badly hurt in hospital, his doormen weren't there for him. When one of the 'runners' tried to cover for his bottle drop Rob's brother stopped him in his tracks, 'there is no excuse,' he said, 'you were either there or you weren't. What I want to know is why aren't you lying in the next bed to my brother?' He had no answer to that.

After the split from his lady and an epic and bloody battle with the police because she refused allow him access to his daughter he was served a court injunction making the ban official. The separation tore the lad apart and, when she started school at four years of age he used to sneak to her school playground at dinner time and, from a safe distance, watch her play. She didn't even know who he was. He was not ashamed to admit to me that he cried his eyes out every time he watched his daughter through the bars of a school fence.

When I first met Rob he had learned his lesson and shed his violent past, he had matured into a talker of repute who could handle any situation placed before him. Rob was a leader, not a follower. A typical example of his 'fighting without fighting' was the night he neutralised a situation in which I was going to 'bury' a guy over an argument about three chicken nuggets. Sounds silly I know, but there was a little more to it than that. On a Wednesday night I used to start work on the door at Buster's straight from teaching my karate class. As you can imagine, this never left me much time to eat, so the first thing I used to do when I arrived at Buster's was order some chicken nuggets from the little 'hole in the wall' café that the club ran. It was a bit of a ritual I had and those nuggets meant a lot to me. I was stood in the reception, eating my food and watching the myriad customers pay entrance to the club. Rob was at the door searching people as they came in.

'Geoff, can you come to the bar, we've got a little problem.' It was Graham, our short, squat glass collector who fancied himself as a budding doorman, though every time it 'kicked off' he ran for the anonymity of being a glass collector again. He was one of those guys that looked as though they'd been squashed, a bit like the 'fat reflection' in one of those fairground mirrors. He fancied the 'fame' of bouncing, the women groupies, the respect and the kudos but didn't realise that these things came at a price that most are not prepared to pay. There's a price tag attached to most things in life. He even went as far as convincing the management that they should allow him a spot on the infamous Buster's door. John said that he wasn't fit to open the door let alone stand on it. One night, just to make his point, John sent Graham into the club to sort out an 'altercation'. He told him that there was a monster playing up at the bar, 'go and get him out for me Graham, let's see what you're made of!' This was his big chance and he was determined to prove himself. He walked towards the bar, arms splayed like he was carrying an invisible fridge under each . . . but never got past the toilets half way up the club. His bowels deserted him like rats from a sinking ship. 'What did I tell ya?' was John's comment. There was no monster causing trouble by the bar. John had made it up. 'I rest my case,' John said to the manager. 'Just because the lad wants to do the door doesn't mean that he can do it.'

Reluctantly I left my nuggets under the watchful eye of 'Eric' the cashier and followed Graham to the bar. While I was at the bar one of the customers, a tall heavy set student with a Scottish tang walking through reception, nicked two of my nuggets. The cheek of the lad.

'Don't touch the nuggets,' the receptionist said, too late, 'they're the doorman's.'

The lad smiled, like she had thrown him a challenge, and took another nugget before entering the club. Don't you just want to kill him already? To him it may have been little more than a university prank where kudos points are collated by being 'daring'. In the university of life, or more specifically Buster's night club, pranks such as this could dramatically change the course of your life. I have to say that some of these students didn't have a fucking clue about the real world and how dangerous it could be. One stood in front of me one night, after attacking me with the most offensive verbal onslaught I have ever heard and said, poking my chest,

'Go on then, hit me!' Big smile on his face, a sardonic nod of the head, a taunting laugh. 'You can't can you, because that would be against the law?'

BANG!! I knocked him clean out with a right that was cut just for him. He hit the deck like a heavy thing. I looked down at him unconscious on the floor and said,

'You don't know Coventry very well, do ya?' When I returned from the bar — the incident was a silly dispute over the price of beer — I realised that someone had taken my nuggets. I was fuming. I felt like baby bear coming back to find my porridge 'all gone', except that my goldilocks wasn't a sweet little child with a tummy rumble it was a big, ugly Scot with an attitude.

'Who's had me nuggets?' I asked, sure that the staff were playing a trick on me or that Rob had shoved them into one of the many coat pockets in the cloakroom.

'Eric' (the receptionist that looked like Eric Bristow — remember?) looked at me and said,

'I told him that they were yours but he didn't take any notice.'

'Who?' I was mad already.

'That guy in the club there.' She leaned over the counter and pointed to the tall Scots guy just inside the club. I bounded through the double glass doors that separated the reception from the club and strode purposefully into the noisy club. I made a bee line for the nugget thief and tapped him aggressively on the shoulder like I was trying to make a hole in his shirt.

'I hear you're the guy that stole my nuggets?'

He laughed, which kind of infuriated me even more.

'Yea, sorry about that. I didn't know they were yours.'

I lined him up, ready for the fight, just in case.

'You knew they were mine, the girl told you and you still took them.'

'Oh,' he lied, smiling like a cheshire cat that had just stole the cream (or was it cheese?), 'I thought she was joking.'

'Well she wasn't joking and now you owe me six chicken nuggets.' He'd only stolen three but I was keen to make a profit.

'No, I'm not buying you any nuggets. I didn't know they were yours.'

It was as much as I could do to keep my hands off the guy. No one should get between a man and his chicken, shag his wife, beat his children but hey 'don't touch the nuggets'. I was absolutely fuming.

'I'll tell you what I'll do, I'll give you five minutes to get me a plate of nuggets. If they're not in reception in five minutes then I'm coming for you.' I poked his chest to drive home the point. Fucking wanker! Who'd he think he was nicking my dinner? In retrospect I can't believe I was getting ready to batter a guy over a plate of nuggets. But what else could I do? If people have so little respect for me that they can steal my dinner and then laugh in my face what kind of a doorman am I?

Imagine the scenario if you will: you're out with your lady (or man), you're sitting in a restaurant in town with a lovely meal in front of you that you've looked forward to all day. 'Hello,' you think, 'I need a wee'. 'Scuse me m'darlin, m'love, gotta go where the big nobs hang out.' You nip to the loo to make room for your next few drinks only to come back and find a guy digging into your dinner. Well what are you gonna do? (Bearing in mind that 99% of my mates have already ripped his arms and legs off.) Are you going to let him have it? Well, are you? I didn't think so. Personally I just couldn't let it go. For the moment I left it at that. I walked back into the reception and started counting down the minutes. 'Eric' had already filled Rob in about the missing nuggets and I told them both of the five minute ultimatum.

'If my dinner isn't on this table in five minutes I'm gonna beat that guy a new face!'

Rob looked concerned. He knew me well enough to know that when the five minutes were up I was going to be fighting. I remember the time I was trying to help him stop ten guys from beating each other to death outside the club, it wasn't that heavy but the lads had to be stopped. Rob was trying to pull one group apart and I the other. I dragged one bloke out three times, only for him to run back in and dig someone again. When I grabbed him the third time I said, 'Look I don't want to fight with you but if you don't fuck off and stop fighting I'm gonna have to.' He took a lot of no notice and dived back in again. When I grabbed him for the fourth time he turned and went for me. BANG! I hit him with a little right, just enough to calm him down and he hit the deck like an unconscious thing. I walked towards one of the others still fighting and said, 'You too. You'd better stop as well!' Another nob who wouldn't let me talk. BANG! Another short right — not so hard this time, I just wanted to shock him so that he would stop fighting — another KO. He hit the deck next to his mate and they looked like 'bed mates'. Rob didn't see any of this, he was too busy trying to sort the other lot out, and I didn't tell him. After it was all over we sat in the manager's office, Rob put on the video recorder, he wanted to see how the situation had started. I stood at the back of the room watching past the heads of the other doormen and the manager. When it came to the bit with me knocking out the two guys Rob said, 'Fuck! I wondered who sparked them.' I went red with embarrassment. I didn't even mean it.

Five minutes was ticking away slowly. Rob looked across at me, he splayed his arms and shrugged his shoulders.

'Geoff, it's only a plate of nuggets!'

'Yea. Well what if they were your nuggets Rob, what would you do? Let the wanker have them. I don't think so.'

'Yea, you're right. But don't be too hasty Geoff, let me have a word with the lad.' Rob approached the Scot who seemed in no hurry to get to the café for my dinner. I stayed in reception and thought about the consequences of my intended actions. I imagined myself up before the judge and charged with 'killing a nugget thief', the judge looking down at me in condemnation, rubbing his chin in a confused manner and saying, 'Now, run this by me again Mr Thompson, you killed this man because he stole three chicken nuggets from you?' Then, slamming his judicial hammer on his desk, 'Take him down!' I could see myself in the maximum security wing of some hard core jail talking to some monster armed robber with a face like a caveman's ugly club. 'What are you in for?' I'd ask. 'Killed a guy for raping my wife, what about you?' 'Me? I killed a guy for nicking three chicken nuggets off me!' Doesn't sound too good, does it?

Rob cornered the thief by the bar and went to work.

'Are you going to get Geoff his nuggets?'

'Naw. I didn't even know they were his. I shouldn't have to buy him another lot. This is just silly, he's taking it too personally.' Rob could see that the lad was adamant and that he obviously didn't realise he was going to be fighting for his life in a few minutes if he didn't get an order in at the café soon. He went for the psyche. He had to say something that would make this wanker realise that I was serious and that, for £1's worth of nuggets, it was hardly worth it. He made his play.

I was stood impatiently by reception when Rob walked back down carrying a plate full of steaming hot nuggets, bought by my Scottish friend. I was non-plussed, I felt pretty sure that I was going to have to fight for them. Rob laid out the scenario: the lad was adamantly not going to reimburse me until Rob had explained to him that, having just finished conducting a gruelling karate class, teaching some of the country's finest martial artists how to 'fuck' other human beings (Rob's description not mine), I was pretty fucking ravished and not in the mood for 'nugget thieves'.

'How would you feel,' Rob asked him, 'if you'd just finished a hard karate session and some guy steals your dinner?'

'He does karate?' Scott asked, the fear starting to grip his voice like a clamp.

'Oh yea, didn't you know? One of the best in the country.'
'WAITER! A PLATE FULL OF YOUR BEST NUGGETS IF YOU PLEASE. AND BE QUICK ABOUT IT!'

Apparently after hearing the word 'karate' the lad couldn't get his 'nugget' order in quick enough. That was Rob, and the art of fighting without fighting as Mr Lee might have said.

Talking about training, I had a beautiful young lady teaching me karate every Thursday for a year because she thought I was too soft for the job and needed some help. I was actually a second dan in Shotokan at the time, but I didn't tell her that, she thought I was a novice and as a yellow belt she could 'help me out'.

'Will you teach me that karate stuff then?' I asked. 'I get really scared on the door and I'm sure it will help.' The lads were in bits as this young curvaceous thing with sparkling eyes wrapped herself around me in a bid to teach me 'the moves' every week. She showed me how to throw a punch and a kick and how to block an attack. I did my very best to make my efforts really bad to hide my skill and she did her best, very tactiley, to correct me.

'I worry about you, Geoff,' she told me one night, mid way through the lesson in the reception area of the club. 'I've been showing you these moves now for quite some time and you just don't seem to be picking them up at all. I don't know what you're gonna do if you get into a fight. You're just too nice.'

'Yes,' I agreed, trying not to split my sides laughing, 'I'm worried too, and the other doormen bully me which doesn't help matters.' She threw a disapproving glance at the other doormen as though to say, 'leave the poor man alone, you can see how soft he is'. As she gave me a comforting cuddle —

she smelled of *Chanel* — John shook his head in mock disgust. Colin raced into the cloakroom and buried his head into the coats hanging on the rail to stifle his gagging laughter. This went on for ages and ages and I really looked forward to my weekly lessons from this beautiful young lady — until one Thursday night when she came into the club and glared over like she wanted to kill me. The game was up.

'What's the matter?' I asked, already backing into the club.

'You bastard!'

'Pardon?' I was shocked. I back peddled some more.

'Bastard!' she repeated as she ran at me like a demented thing. I legged it into the club crying with laughter as she raced after me throwing insults and beer mats and whatever else she could get her hands on. The other doormen were rolling around the floor with laughter. Turns out there was a big article in the local paper about me winning a karate competition and me being a high graded karataka, and when she read it she realised that I'd been stringing her along for nearly a year. She was fuming. Ah well, it was nice whilst it lasted, though it goes without saying that my Thursday night lessons ended forthwith.

8. The Adrenal Map

Fear: one of the most important and profound lessons that I learned whilst working the doors — a real gem of knowledge — was that fear never goes away. Those who try to shed it like an old suit of clothing or cure it like an illness always end up disappointed beyond belief. Those who try to analyse and rationalise it usually become confused and subsequently more afraid than before. Why? Because when it fails to 'shed' and when it refuses to 'heal' they feel as though they've failed. Then they become more afraid of fear than they were in the first place. They feel that not only has it defeated them in the arena but they are also doomed to live under its dominion for the rest of their lives. Some never quite recover from the defeat. But they haven't failed, except in not realising that they had chased the wrong dream.

The sense of fear is the body's early warning system, it's a notification of forthcoming danger. The mechanics of fear are the body's natural turbo drive that can, and do, vehicle you painlessly and speedily away from or through adversity. So I ask 'Why on earth would you want to 'shed' something so primary to your own survival?' Because it's uncomfortable? If it didn't hurt what kind of holocaust would this world become with everyone seeking adversity because fear felt 'nice?' So the trick is not expecting a painless ride, rather it is in anticipating just that and even practising with friends and loved ones so that when it does happen you are not so ill prepared. But to do that, to confront the things that we fear most takes self power, the ability to get yourself to do the things that you fear most to do, because that is where real power lies, not in getting others to do our bidding but in getting ourselves to.

During the third scene in *Lawrence Of Arabia*, arguably the most splendidly shot film of all time, the leading character dowses a lit match with his fingers. Intrigued by his lack of discomfort, another soldier 'Potter' tries imitating the feat, with painful results. 'Ouch! It damn well hurts!' 'Certainly it hurts,' replies Lawrence. 'Well, what's the trick then?' asks the soldier. 'The trick, Mr Potter, is not minding that it hurts.'

Fear is a big part of working the doors and if you can't handle it, if you don't understand it, it'll absolutely fuck you up. I've lost count of the number of people I've seen who lost their bottle in a real fight because they didn't understand their own bodies and the disguises of fear. And, even if you are the only recipient of exposure, the 'ripples' of adrenal 'splash' can effect everyone who works/lives with you in what is fast becoming an increasingly confrontational job/world.

Here's a little piece I wrote at the beginning of my book *Fear — The Friend Of Exceptional People*. It explains nicely my thoughts on and about fear in the 20th century:

'Working one's way through a life that is fraught with intangible confrontation, in an adrenal loaded body that was better designed for conflicts of the tangible kind, fight or flight, it is small wonder that most people do go to their graves with their best songs still in them. For the adrenal syndrome, that was better suited to the mortal conflict of fighting or escaping the sabre toothed tiger, is lost in a decade where confrontation may be a boardroom meeting, high mortgage rates or a row with the spouse.

Tangible confrontation on a base level, where the adrenal rush adds speed, power and anaesthesia to response, has been succeeded by confrontations of a rather translucent nature, a run-in with the boss, or perhaps a business decision. In the latter scenarios adrenalin is released but not utilised because neither fight nor flight is an option. It would be unreasonable and anti-

social (though often damned tempting) to strike a vindictive boss and unwise (though very common) to run away from confrontations in the home. So one often finds oneself infused with unrecognised and un-utilised adrenalin. The subsequent inner pressure eventually explodes like the cork of a shaken champagne bottle, usually unexpectedly and often without warning or provocation, into tamer parts of our lives.

Concurrently the reasoning process, misreading the feeling of adrenalin for fear, builds a subconscious periphery that imprisons the part of us that wants to achieve. Fear is what keeps people ordinary.

It is said that knowledge dispels fear. Have a good look around you, also have a good look at yourself. How many people do you know who are truly happy with their lot? Society is full of under achievers, and not because we lack potential, nor courage, rather we lack an understanding of our own bodily reactions to confrontation. Because of this, adrenalin often catalyses panic, forcing a possible abortion of plans to change, expand, explore etc for fear of consequence or often for fear of fear itself.

Twenty-five centuries ago General Sun Tzu said, 'if you know your enemy and know yourself you need not fear the outcome of a hundred battles'. Knowing yourself is understanding that the enemy is often within and that society is the battlefield.

Through my own search and experimentation I have learned that the explosion inside the stomach that so many people struggle with and that causes the infamous 'freeze' syndrome which begets defeat is adrenalin.

In primeval times when mankind had to fight to live and eat, the feeling of fear was an every day occurrence that would have felt as natural and as common as eating or drinking. In today's society, where confrontation is less tangible and less usual, the act of fighting or running for our lives is no longer a part of every day living, so when a situation arises that causes the adrenalin to flow, and because we are so unfamiliar with it (unlike our pre-historic ancestors) we, naturally, neither welcome, use or like it (we panic). Psychologists call it the 'Fight or Flight' syndrome. In moments of danger/confrontation the body releases a chemical (adrenalin) from the adrenal gland that hits and goes through the blood-stream like a speeding train, preparing the body for 'fight or flight', deeming it stronger, faster and partially, sometimes completely, anaesthetised to pain. The more demanding the situation the bigger the build-up and adrenalin release, the bigger the release the better the performance (run, fight), but by the same count, the bigger the build-up and release, the harder it is to control.

Subsequently, because the adrenalin often lies un-utilised in the body it builds up, like a pressure cooker, and explodes in other aspects of our lives, ie. in the car, road-rage, or in the home, shouting at the wife/husband/children etc.'

On the door you get adrenalin every single night of the week — though it often comes in different ways — but only on a small number of those occasions does the adrenalin actually get used. Most of the situations you are confronted by in your capacity as a doorman do not demand either fight or flight, subsequently you end up stuck with a body full of adrenalin that you don't need. This surplus has to be utilised somewhere along the line and if you don't do something about it the body will find its own way of expelling it from the system. I remember as a young, inexperienced doorman smashing my whole house up in unprovoked outbursts of violence (I hit doors — never people) that could be triggered by the slightest thing. My wife — ex-wife now (yea, yea I know) — used to say that I was a 'fucking nutcase' to quote the phrase. Which was pretty rich coming from a lady who blacked my eyes more than my sparring partners and who used to get fan mail from the Gestapo (but that's a different story). I couldn't tell her why my actions were so irrational nor what had caused my unforgivable behaviour. I couldn't tell her because I didn't know myself, I was starting to think that perhaps she was right, maybe I was a 'fucking nutcase' — I was turning into a monster.

It was only later, a while later, after much experience in 'the arena' that I learned to understand my body and began to realise what was happening to me — this helped me greatly in controlling and excreting the unused adrenalin that ran round my body like a hoard of flies trapped in a jam jar. I also watched my fellow doormen and the fighters that they, and I, had to deal with on a daily basis. I came to the realisation that adrenalin often came in different ways, what I call the disguises of fear, and the fellows that didn't understand these disguises were the ones most likely to 'drop their bottle' in a confrontation — any confrontation. These unfortunates were then seen, by their peers and certainly by themselves, as cowards — but they were not cowards, they were just uninitiated people, tricked by their own bodily reactions to varying genres of confrontation.

This in mind, I formulated the adrenal map which detailed all the disguises of fear so that one could understand and better control the beast within and also use the information to beat an opponent, with guile as opposed to force, by triggering his own adrenalin against him. This is what I came up with: **Think-confrontation fear.** This is what you feel when you anticipate confrontation. The body releases adrenalin slowly and often over a long period. The slow release is not so intense as the fast release but, due to its longevity, it can wear and corrode the recipient. Things like anticipation of having to talk in public, an exam, a big sales meeting, a forthcoming karate competition, a planned confrontation with the husband/wife/neighbour/boss/bully etc. will cause slow release, anything from seconds to months before the expected confrontation.

This was one of the hardest things about working the doors. You may have a queue of people waiting to come into the club and half way down that queue stands a monster in training shoes that you know you're going to have to turn away. You also know that he's gonna want to fight you because of it. It might take twenty minutes for him to reach the front of the queue so you have to handle that baby — think fight fear — for twenty minutes. A long time when your knees are doing the bosanova.

On other occasions you suddenly find that you have a gang of men in the club that are going to kick off, but you don't know when, and you are on the edge experiencing a whole night of think fight, and fuck me does that take it out of you. I remember a night such as this when we'd had the word that a big fight was gonna 'go down' between two rival gangs in Buster's night club, one of which was congregating near the reception doors. The atmosphere in the club had been bad all night and the doormen had sensed that something might kick off. Call it intuition, a sixth sense, I don't know what it was, but we all felt it and knew that something was going to happen. It was still early, about a quarter to midnight and people were busily coming and going from the club. There was a big crowd in, about usual for a Friday night and they were all forming little groups by the doors, the bar, and on the edge of the dance floor. Not a good sign. It was as though they were preparing for a battle.

No worries, we had the best door in the city and were confident that we could handle any eventualities. This team was a rarity; every doorman could have a fight and the bond we had developed through the keen leadership of Awesome Anderson was unquestionable. Even the other door teams in the city acknowledged our prowess. It had never taken a loss even though teams from every part of the city had chanced their arm — they all came out a very sorry second place. A job on the door of Buster's meant, in bouncer terms, you had made it — we were the élite and no one fucked, well not twice anyway.

Now, there's two things you can do with this baby — though you don't always have the choice — one is to take charge and confront the situation early and get rid of it. Waiting for a confrontation is like carrying a monkey on your back and the more you leave the situation the fatter the monkey gets, until he gets too heavy to carry.

The second solution is to sit and wait for it to happen. The latter is the solution that many take because, at the time, it probably feels easier than actually confronting it. Waiting for a fight to kick off is like coming home from the pub after 15 pints of Pils, three curries and a bumpy taxi ride, you know you're going to be sick, you just know it! But what do you do? You climb into bed — once the room stops spinning — and try to ignore it, you even drink loads of water to try and dilute it, in short you do everything you can to avoid being sick. Then, after three hours of agony tossing and turning in bed you rush to the toilet and shout your mate 'Huighy' for fifteen minutes and find things in your vomit that you know you didn't eat. Which reminds me of the time when one of my friends was sick in his neighbour's back garden — better than being sick in your own I suppose — he looked down through blurred eyes at what remained of £40 and a good night out, and his vomit started to move, honestly. Slowly but surely it walked across the garden — strange but true. Sure that he was hallucinating he screamed and ran for the sanctuary of his bed. He didn't tell anyone of his ordeal for fear they might think him mad, but he nearly choked laughing the next night when he over heard his neighbour complaining, 'some fucking thoughtless bastard was sick all over my Tortoise last night. Would you believe it?'.

The best thing to do when you know you are going to be sick is stick you fingers down your throat and save yourself hours of pain and misery. It's the same with violence. You don't want it to happen and you try every which way to avoid it but at the end of the day it's going to happen so, metaphorically speaking, you might as well slam your fingers down your throat and get it over with. Sometimes of course you can't do that. A boxer, for instance, has to handle think fight for months before a fight and there is no way that he can bring the fight forward and end his misery. So he just has to handle it. We'll talk about that in a bit. But, if you do have the choice then take my advice and 'get the monkey off your back'.

I've had a few times in my life where the voice on the phone has said 'when I see ya I'm gonna kill ya!' And I've replied, 'Oh Really? Is that right? Where are ya right now, give me the address and I'll meet ya now and you can have a shot!' The voice becomes hesitant, unsure, this wasn't in his fight plan. 'No, no. I'll see you sometime.' 'See me now and we'll do it. I'll fucking change the course of your life.' No takers!! That might sound like I'm being a brave bastard. Not really, in actuality I'm taking the easiest of the two options and getting the monkey off my back.

When I got jumped in a night club one night by a gang, and the other doormen I was working with did a 'runner', the main man in the gang told me that he was 'coming back for me!' I followed him and three of his mates out of the night club and confronted him. I won't go into the details because the story is in *Watch My Back* but basically I didn't want the monkey on my back so I did it there and then, I said 'Hey, I want a word.' All four of them turned to face me. 'You were such a big mouth in there. How about me and you, around the corner now?' He went pale and was gobsmacked. 'No, man, I can't guarantee my safety around here. Your mates you know.' His feeble excuse angered me. 'What fucking mates? They've locked me out.' (The other doormen had locked the doors behind me.) He looked at the closed door, then back to me. His mates turned away: now it was just him and me. He was alone. He tried to maintain his cool but his fear shone like a neon light. 'No man, another time.' I was going to hit him but humiliation would hurt him more. 'Never mind another time,' I said rubbing salt into the wound, 'now, me and you. Leave your mates here and and we'll go around the corner and do it.' He shook his head and disappeared up his own arsehole. This wasn't really about being a brave bastard it was about making a choice, now or later, by taking control I was saving myself hours, days, even weeks of unnecessary anticipation.

In this particular scenario (back at Buster's with the two rival gangs — if I lost you there) we did have a choice. We knew the troublemakers — there were about ten of them, ominously standing several feet away from us — so decided to nip the trouble in the bud. If we let it go and just waited for the inevitable it might have grown to monstrous proportions, so we wanted to catch the apple at the seed.

I moved towards the main man in the gang while John shadowed me. The music was blaring in the background, some guy called Meatloaf was screaming something about a 'bat out of hell', and cigarette smoke attacked my eyes like a thousand ex-wives — at least it wasn't going for the bollocks, the house, the car, half your wages . . . that kind of scenario.

'Lads, you'll have to move into the club. Sorry about that. Move into the club, please, you're blocking the entrance doors.'

The lad blanked me. I expected as much, in fact I hoped he would because I needed an excuse to get him out of the club and if it was going to 'kick' then it was better to be pro-active than reactive.

'DID YOU HEAR ME? MOVE INTO THE CLUB OR YOU'LL HAVE TO GO!' I made my point and made it load. Every one of them moved quickly into the club, all but one. A little ginger haired wanker with a painted-on grimace that was looking to be knocked off. I approached him. He turned his back to me. I was in no mood for playing the subliminal challenge game. He was obviously the leader of the pack (sorry about that Gary) and all his mates looked on from in the club to see what he was going to do. John and the other doormen watched my back. This was it, this was the spark that could ignite the explosion but at least I was holding the match.

I was quiet again. I knew that this man was in charge of the other nine and I also knew that if I could get rid of him we could calm the others, in controlling him we would automatically control them. By standing alone and refusing to move into the club at my instruction he had highlighted himself as the main man. Really he was just another fucking pleb on a Saturday night ego trip. But he was playing games in absolutely the wrong place. He was what Harry Cook might have called the mouse playing by the hawks' nest.

'You have to move into the club.'

He sipped his beer, looked at me, smiled a sardonic smile then looked away again. The deaf and dumb tactic was often used to psyche out an inexperienced player. It was fucking kindergarten stuff and the guy was an amateur at that. I was insulted that he thought himself up to 'playing the game' with me. I let my distaste show and took the game up a league to see how he handled it. So far the nob hadn't even spoken, for all I knew he could have been a deaf mute (no disrespect to deaf mutes of course).

'Fucking move into the club or you're leaving!'

'Who says?' He stepped up the league with me. His question was his way of making it personal and taking the 'interview' to its limit.

'I say.' This was my way of saying I'll get as personal as you fucking like.

He pointed at my chest.

'You personally?'

It was a skilful manoeuvre and one that has been used on me by many players before, it was an ace card. In one sentence, with one question he had taken away my whole back-up. He had also taken away his own back-up as well, of course. More psyche. He was now saying, 'not me and my mates, not you and the other doormen, me and you'. He was offering me a way out, and many doormen take the exit at this point because they know they are on their own, and against a name fighter that's a very lonely place to be because when you take him on alone, you are not just engaging a three second fight you're taking on a possible lifetime enemy.

When I fought Mr G in the Red Lion pub (story in *Bouncer*) I didn't just take on a ten second physical encounter. That would have been relatively easy. I knew I could take him — and do a good job at that — but I also knew that, after his defeat, I'd have an enemy for life. He petrol bombed the last pub that I worked in and also petrol bombed the cars of at least two men who had crossed his path. So what I had to take into account was the fact that every time this wanker looked in the mirror and saw gums where he should have seen teeth he would remember me and the time that I kicked them down his violent throat with a pair of Fila trainers and twenty years of practice on the punch bag. Every time he had a row with his lady and his life hit a low and every time the drink made him think he could 'take me' there'd be a chance of him turning up on my doorstep with a can of petrol and a match. Every time this wanker saw me in the street for the rest of my life there would be a fair chance that he'd try and marry me with six inches of steel, or if he really got on a death wish he might do what he threatened on the night and end my life with a barrel full of lead. Fighting people like this is not a ten second encounter, it's a lifetime commitment.

In short, Ginger was playing the same game, he was trying to psyche me out by making it personal but it wasn't happening for him. I was already totally committed to getting him out of the club, horizontal or vertical — the choice was very much his. He was hoping at this point that, having successfully taken away my back-up — the other doormen — that I may have 'declined his offer' to get 'intimate'. I looked him hard in the face.

'Yea, me personally. I want you out. Not the other doormen, not the manager. Me personally.'

I snatched at his glass of beer and he pulled back hard so I grabbed him by the back of his hair and started dragging him to the door. His mates made a futile movement forward and John stopped them with a single stare. One did step forward, almost apologetically to defend his mate. He shouldn't have, he was out of his depth. John grabbed him round the neck in a choke and held him there like a child.

'You're leaving!' he said, then looked at the rest of the crew who were already melting back into the crowd of night club revellers like apparitions. 'Anyone else want to go?'

No answer.

'If you start any more trouble in the club I won't let you leave. I'll close the doors and send you home in boxes.'

The whole crowd gulped in unison. John had a way of convincing people that it wasn't a good idea to cross him. I once watched a guy pull a baseball bat on him at the door of Buster's. John looked the bat up and down and said, 'I'll let you keep the bat. It'll make it even.' He dropped the bat, along with his bottle and ran for his mother.

Towards the door Ginger started to struggle violently so I tightened my grip. He looked up at me — I was holding him by the hair at about waist height — his face was red with rage and he was kind of snorting like an angry bull.

'I'll be back for you,' he snarled, 'no one else, just you personally. I'll find out where you live, you bastard, and I'll be back.' OK Arnie!

'Is that right?' I said, struggling to hide my anger. 'You're not in a great position to be throwing threats.'

'I'll fucking well be back!'

'Don't bother coming back,' I said, cocking my left hand for an uppercut, 'let's do it now.'

Bang! Bang! Bang! I didn't see any sense in trying to keep on the lad's good side. Three left hands in the head and he flew into the closed front doors of the club like he'd been fired from a catapult. As he bounced off his head was about my waist height and I did the only thing a man could do in that situation: I kicked him in the face with a technique I'd practised a million times on the bag. His front teeth flew out and his eye closed into a big purple plum. He tumbled out of the door and onto the pavement. Twenty people who were queueing outside '*oohed*' as he hit the deck in an unconscious heap. They all looked at each other as though to say, 'And we're paying to come in here?'.

'My name's Geoff Thompson. When you come back ask for me personally.' I don't know why I said that, the guy was unconscious and hardly responsive. Still, someone would pass the message on I was sure. John was right behind me and flung Ginger's associate out by the neck. He landed pathetically on top of his sleeping mate. Once we had removed the source of trouble we enjoyed a relatively quiet night with no occurrences from Ginger's mob. The monkey had well and truly been removed.

Turns out that Ginger was a school teacher who'd caused riots at many of the other night clubs in the city and had enacted some terrible glassings. Most of the people hurt in these affrays are innocents, our sons and daughters out for a good time. This wanker liked to start gang fights in his spare time like an arsonist likes to start fires but they forget that it is not a game and at some point they are going to get burned themselves. What I want to know is how the fuck does a man like this get to become a school teacher? These people are teaching our children!? Hopefully he learned a lesson that night, as far as I know he never started any trouble again after that. I heard the lad settled down a little so maybe I did him and the rest of the city a favour? Sometimes a good hiding can put a bird back on the right path. I think, not wanting to sound pretentious, that we were perhaps his karma. He never visited Buster's again, that much I know for sure. Can't say I was surprised or disappointed!

The way to deal with think fight fear is either to take control and get the monkey off your back — the sooner the better — or, if that's not possible and you have to wait a week for the confrontation, utilise the adrenalin each day with a heavy regime of physical training. Fight or flight is a physical syndrome that needs a physical release. What I do to release mine is hit the bag every day — not so easy now I'm divorced from her (joke) — or go for a long run. Which is also what I advised my ex — I told her that if she ran five miles a day she'd burn of a pound every week, and by Christmas I'd have gotten rid of her completely.

Physical training, especially explosive training, will release the adrenalin until you are ready for confrontation. Also, on long hauls, make sure that you get plenty to eat: food is your fuel. The problem is when adrenalin is on the agenda appetite disappears like a penny down the drain so people stop eating. That's the worst thing you can do because the body thinks there's a famine and starts to feed off itself. First it will use up excess fat stores for energy, then it attacks calories and you'll experience a drop in body weight, then it feeds off protein, which is your muscle mass, then, as a final reserve tank it will work off nervous energy. When it does this you're in the shit. You'll start experiencing massive highs and equally extreme lows. That's when your problems really start and a nervous breakdown is barking at the door like a pack of hungry wolves. So feed the fight, even if you don't feel hungry eat, or there will be no fight. The body is like a car: if you don't fill the tank then you don't take the journey.

Using the adrenalin with a good training session will also enable you to sleep better. Un-utilised adrenalin seems to sit in the body like waste food, if you don't get it out it is very uncomfortable and so, of course, you won't be able to sleep, it hurts, it's like a physical pain and the more you panic with it the worse it gets because you become anxious and the body is fooled into thinking that the anxiety is a sign of more trouble ahead, a bigger confrontation, so it releases more adrenalin for what it believes to be fight or flight. Understand it, nip it in the bud, take control of it. The best thing about all of this is that because you are taking control and getting rid of the psychological shit from your system it's not having to find its own way out. When it finds its own release who do you think gets it? The people you love, that's who, those near and dear.

Before you know it you find yourself in the divorce courts. Your family is very important, you need quality time with them, self utilisation (sounds painful) will allow you this.

One of the biggest causes of 'bottle drop' (sounds like a tropical illness) is what I call Pre-post-fight fear. This is what you get when you anticipate the consequence of confrontation, negative or positive, before it even happens. The fear of that consequence, failure, success, humiliation, comebacks etc often forces the recipient to abort prematurely. This is not just in physical confrontations, it's the same in life. Many people do not achieve their dreams because they worry too much about the consequences of taking a chance. Of course we have to look at the upshot but we shouldn't allow it to scare us off and take away our aspirations.

Pre-post-fight fear is one of the most common things that a doorman has to contend with in his daily life. It occurs especially when faced with a name fighter. It also occurs when one over anticipates comebacks from the law. One of my closest friends badly let me down in a gang fight because of this: he was worried sick about being 'lifted' by the police. I could have died for his fears yet he still couldn't find it in him to help me.

On another occasion a friend took a severe beating from a gang because his back-up disappeared up their own arseholes. Why? Because they were worried about comeback from these 'name' fighters. They just stood there and watched as he got kicked near to death. They were told by the gang 'this is personal, it's nothing to do with you. If you get involved we'll come to your houses and burn them down'. They'd been known to do it in the past so the threat was not an idle one. What do you do? Do you stand there and watch your mate get beaten into the ground to save your own bacon or do you go down fighting with him? From the comfort of your armchair I know you'll be saying 'there's no way I'd bottle it', and I know that you really believe it. But do you? Do you really? Think of the biggest name fighters in your own town, the ones that frighten the shit out of you, place four of them in front of you, giving you the same threat, 'you get involved and we'll come to your house and burn it down'. Then think of who is at your house right now, your mother, your father, maybe your wife and new baby, your little boy, your fiancée? It's all starting to look a bit different now, isn't it?

I've been there and not lost my bottle but believe me it was hard and I have to say that I felt like running. It took every bit of willpower I could summon up to hold me there, I had to accept that these people might kill me. Fucking scarey, let me tell you. When someone tells me that a doorman bottled it and that they would 'never do that' I know one thing for sure, they have never faced real fear. I have never let my friends down but as much as I'd like to say I never would and that I would never lose my bottle I can't, no one can. No one knows how they are going to react until it happens.

Another one of my friends, an absolute fucking monster of a fighter, was stood outside a city gym when a black M3 BMW pulled up alongside him and the smoke glass electric window purred open to reveal a heavy set man wearing a gangster overcoat and looking through hollow eyes that said 'death'. The gangster in the car said to my friend 'Where's Mr B?' It was asked in a calm yet authoritative manner. Mr B was a very close mate of my friend and had been expecting a visit from some heavies that he'd crossed. My mate didn't give a fuck who this man was or how heavy he was meant to be. He was going to defend Mr B to the death if need be, or at least he thought he was. He walked to the car and leant arrogantly toward the passenger window. 'Who the fuck wants to know?' he said challengingly. 'Hollow eyes' slid the shotgun through the window and perched it under my friend's chin. Obviously a determined fellow. 'We do!' My mate's eyes nearly popped out of their sockets and he retreated back to a respectful and safe distance — Birmingham — and said pointing towards the gym, 'I don't know, I think he's in the gym.' Knowing the man you would have bet your house that he wouldn't have said that but if you did you'd be living in a cardboard box right now.

I also watched the Midlands boxing champ get his face beaten off outside a night club by a local heavy who, in physical terms, was not fit to clean his boots, in the ring he wouldn't have even come to scratch, yet he hammered this guy till you couldn't recognise what species he was let alone who he was. The boxer didn't even try to fight back, he was too scared of the consequences of standing up to this monster who was renowned for his comebacks. That's pre-post-fight fear and if you don't understand it it'll hit you like a hammer in the eye. Everyone gets it, some can override it but it takes guts in bucketsfull.

As I said before you don't just take this guy on for the few seconds/minutes it might take to neutralise him, potentially you take the man on for life. On a tangible level, having worked the door for ten years in some pretty fucking horrible places I have felt this fear on many occasions. And, as I have said, the fear was not of actually getting into the arena — more the anticipation and the consequences of violence. Before the fight I would often doubt my own courage (mistaking natural apprehension for fear) and either underestimate my own physical ability or over estimate that of my opponent — especially if he was a fighter with a reputation. Later, as an experienced fighter with many KO's to my name my pre-post-fight fear was of inflicting serious damage on whoever I was up against and the consequences of that — ie. living with his death, going to prison, that sort of scenario. So winning a street fight is by no means the be all and end all of the situation, that's the easy part (if any of it can be classed as easy) when dealing with violent, often criminal people.

I vividly remember as though it were yesterday — hold on — it was only yesterday — a confrontation with a very violent, low life, wanker of a knife merchant in Coventry (all right, I admit it, I don't like the man). He was the brother of a local hard man who was notorious for biting off the noses of anyone who messed with his family. Pretty fucking difficult to wear glasses after that, let me tell you.

One night I was running the door in a place that this guy liked to frequent. It was, shall we say, one of the less salubrious districts of metropolitan Coventry. My adversary — lets call him 'fuck face' — had come to let me know that I was on his patch, he was going to emphasise the point by ramming a broken glass into my face. Now I don't know about you but I think there are more civil ways of making a point than this, but we were in Coventry and these sorts of niceties are common here. I believe that you can now actually take a degree in 'violence' at the local university.

This should have been a straightforward fight on the dance floor or in the car park, but there were other factors that had to be taken into account. My dilemma was that the only way to stop him slicing me a new face and giving me the 'Heidelberg scar' that I didn't want was to be pre-emptive and take the guy off the planet first — something I felt quite capable of doing. I was in good shape, highly trained in combat, and sober. But if I did destroy him, I knew that I'd have to deal with his brother and the gang that he led. The possible consequences were beginning to cause hesitation. I knew that I could take the guy out but I had to weigh up the pros and cons. Although it would only take me a few seconds to destroy him, the aftermath might last months — even years. Fighting a man in a blood and snot brawl is one thing; having him, his family and their gang as dangerous enemies for life is something else.

In situations like this one, and there were many, what I'd do, and do do (if you see what I mean) is look at the worst-case scenario and accept that, should it happen, I could handle it. If I felt that I couldn't handle the consequences, and there is no shame in that, then I'd pull out as gracefully as the circumstances would allow. My ego might be slightly bruised, but the rest of me would still be intact. In this case however, with my mate 'fuck face', both scenarios were equally bad. If I didn't fight him he was going to 'cut' me and take away my door, if I did fight and beat him I'd have to face the consequences, which could be dire.

On reflection I decided to beat the man a new face before he had a chance to rearrange mine. I did just that and the aftermath came in a torrent. Luckily I'm pretty well connected myself so we ended up in a Mexican stand off. We threatened each other by turns, and after a few months things returned to normal. Later I even became friends with his infamous crew. If, however, I hadn't accepted the possible consequences of my actions before the fact and prepared myself accordingly, I probably wouldn't have been equipped to handle their threats. Forewarned is forearmed. Whilst this story is of a violent encounter, the same reasoning process should and can apply in most cases where fear causes indecision, capitulation or inertia.

Then there's what my friend Jim Brown calls 'the WOW factor', this is pre-fight fear; psychologists like to call it 'adrenal dump'. This is a fast release of adrenalin and occurs when anticipation is not present, or a situation escalates unexpectedly fast, causing adrenal dump. This feeling is often so intense that the you freeze in the face of confrontation, the reasoning process mistaking it for sheer terror. This I have to say is the most devastating of all. Adrenal dump often occurs when a confrontation arises that you were not ready or prepared for, usually the same scenarios as those that cause slow release but with no anticipation.

Perhaps, without any preparation, you are confronted by some monster who wants to use your face to flatten the world. There is no real preparation for the wow factor other than to stay switched on at all times and always anticipate trouble. This is not easy to do, you have to find middle ground and stay alert to the possibility of confrontation without paranoia setting in.

The wow factor really can be a bastard and I have seen many excellent people lose their bottle under its exposure. I have a friend — lets call him R — in Birmingham, an excellent scrapper and a fine doorman. He's one of the few people that I really rate as a stand up fighter, the guy has an awesome right hand and would fight anyone who stepped into his world. He was telling me, quite unashamedly, about the time he was driving through the city of Birmingham, taking his dad out for the day. En route he got lost and, unsure of the area, he stopped opposite a group of five Indian lads to ask directions.

''scuse me lads,' R shouted across to the group, 'any idea where we are? How I can get to the centre from here. We're lost?'

Within seconds all five of them had surrounded his car. The leader, a heavy set chap with a bad attitude and a cloth crash helmet poked his head through the driver's window (which was funny because it wasn't open at the time).

'I'll fucking tell you where you are mate, you're on our patch and we don't like white people on our patch.'

WHOOSH!! R felt his adrenalin hit overdrive and before he could capture it and command the flow it had raced through his veins with avengeance. He was gobsmacked, he didn't know what to do or say. This was completely unexpected, as he said to me, 'I was out with my dad for fuck's sake, I didn't expect to be getting into any trouble. We only stopped for directions!'

'H-hold on lads, what's the crack? I don't want any trouble. I've just stopped for directions.' The lads started kicking and rocking the car as though trying to tip it over. R quickly rammed it into reverse and sped away with the five men chasing violently after him. Afterwards, at first, he felt ashamed. He felt as though he'd let himself down. 'My bottle just went Geoff,' he told me. 'It's the first time it's ever happened. I can't understand it. If that was on the door I'd have levelled the lot of them.' On the door he would have levelled them because that was an arena he knew like the back of his hand, an arena that he automatically switched on for every night of the week. Outside, in the car with his father, he didn't feel as though he needed to be switched on and when the confrontation hit him he just didn't expect it — in fact it was the very last thing he expected. I explained to him about the disguises of fear and in particular adrenal dump and the fact that, if not prepared, anyone will/can/does lose their bottle. In fact I told him it is not even like losing your bottle it is just being tricked by your own body. If this is not fully understood then suddenly, because of one bad incident, you start doubting yourself, and self doubt can be the beginning of the end. My advice helped him: I don't think he'll be tricked like that again.

Secondary adrenalin is pretty similar to this, only it usually occurs after a situation has finished, when you switch off and go into a kind of celebratory state. Then, for whatever reason, it kicks off again and you get adrenal dump because you were just not prepared. A bit like picking up a firework that has failed to go off, then just when you think it's a dud the fucking thing explodes taking the ends of your fingers off. When a situation that you thought was over re-ignites the unpreparedness gives the body a second kick of adrenalin that is nearly always misread for fear. You've heard the story about the guy who got mugged twice in one night, the first time he battered his attacker the second time he lost his bottle because having already been mugged once he switched his awareness off, as he said afterwards, 'No one gets mugged twice in one night.'

A guy approached the door of a club that my friend was working. He was wearing a heavy trench coat and was scruffier than a scarecrow. My friend refused him entry to the pub on account of his apparel. 'Wurzel', unhappy about being turned away, pulled a sawn-off from under his trench coat like a calling card and said,

'This gets me into any pub in the town'.

My friend hid his fear well and said,

'It doesn't get you into here!' Brave bastard.

'Wurzel' smiled, looked him up and down then placed the gun back under his coat.

'Fair play to ya!' he said and went on his merry little way.

My friend, relieved that it was all over, went into the pub and downed a quick half in celebration. He was a star. Everyone was congratulating him on how brave he was, and talked all night about the spectacle. He was the bravest man in the world. As far as my mate was concerned that was it, nothing could surpass facing a shotgun and he switched off for the night. He experienced a huge injection of endorphene, a natural bodily morphine that the body releases after adversity, and he felt as high as a kite. Towards the end of the night another little incident occurred with a youth by the bar and my mate tried to calm the situation. The youth, a nobody with a thirst for a fight, told my mate to 'fuck off!' When he tried to throw him out for his insolence the youth offered my friend a 'square go' on the car park and he fell apart, his bottle went and in a hurry. What a paradox. No one could believe what they were hearing. The guy that stood up to the gunman bottled it to the little wanker who wanted only fisticuffs. That's secondary adrenalin. It occurs when you lose your zanshin — your awareness — after the fight. So stay switched on until you get home, lock the door of your semi and crack open a bottle of Bud from the fridge and some smoky bacon crisps from the cupboard. That's the time to switch off.

Peripheral adrenalin is another doozy — the name makes it sound complicated; really it's not, it's something that you've probably all experienced at one time or another. It's another sneaky little disguise that grabs many and metaphorically kicks their butt. It usually occurs when awareness is tunnelled. Let me try to explain. When I separated Mr G from his teeth (story in *Bouncer*) he threatened to come down to the pub I worked the next night and shoot me full of holes. He certainly had a rep for dirty deeds so I had to take him at his word. The mistake I made with this baby was over-anticipation. Whilst I needed to prepare myself for the worst case scenario it shouldn't have been to the detriment of everything else. All I could, and did, focus on was Mr G. I thought I was aware, and I was, but my awareness was tunnelled.

While waiting for him to come to the pub, my eyes fixed firmly on the front doors for a very long night, I forgot that there were another two hundred people in the bar who needed monitoring. My lack of peripheral awareness nearly cost me dearly. Suddenly, from out of the periphery a situation exploded: a total arsehole kicked of with a guy right in front of me. When I grabbed the lad to stop him he pulled back violently,

'Get your fucking hands off me you **nt. Get them off!!'

WHOOSH!!!!! Adrenal dump hit me like a hammer in the eye and my arse started to go. Not because I was afraid of this lowlife, but because I had failed to anticipate him because of my tunnelled awareness, I had allowed the situation to take me by surprise. I have to tell you that whilst I did get the guy out of the pub it took every ounce of experience and savvy that I could muster to pull it together and captain my bottle. It was a lesson learned and I never let it happen again, but all the same my bottle nearly went. And after all that Mr G, the toothless wanker, never turned up for our rendezvous. Peripheral adrenalin! Look out for it, it's dynamite.

Once a situation becomes live that caustic feeling we associate with fear usually disappears because the adrenalin is being used. If, however, during confrontation you stumble and things are not going to plan, the brain, again sensing danger, offers a second kick of a adrenalin, in-fight fear, to help you out. This offering is usually misread for fear and panic once again ensues. The in-fight release is there to help you out of a shitty situation or to offer anaesthesia if you are hurt. How many times have you watched two guys having a row and then, suddenly and for no apparent reason, one of them loses his bottle? You think to yourself, 'what happened? He was doing so well'. What happened was he got an injection of in-fight adrenalin that he misread for fear. That's also why, quite often, one blow finishes a fight. It is not that the blow was a finishing strike in itself, it's the fact that the said blow released the adrenalin that the recipient mistook for fear.

You can also get in-post fight fear, which is basically worrying, during the fight, about the consequences afterwards, so much so that it causes mass inertia and loses the guy the fight. I know of one man in the city that uses in-fight fear to psyche out any opponent that takes him the distance. He talks to them during the fight and tells them that he's 'connected' and that, after the fight, win or lose, his team will be visiting his house to burn it down. The amount of people this cheeky lad has beaten with this ploy is unreal — that's in-post fight fear. As an experienced fighter I will and do use this ploy myself. If I want to bottle a guy out, in-fight, I'll give him some pain — usually a head strike — knowing that my attack will spark his adrenalin and he'll, hopefully, mistake it for fear and capitulate. If he doesn't bottle out and the adrenalin causes him to 'buck and brink' I'll be ready for that too. If the latter is the case the lad will use up all his fuel in seconds and be a veritable punch bag thereafter. Exhaustion makes cowards of most men.

Post-confrontation fear, aftermath: this baby fucks up more doormen than the late nights and the booze, because, usually, it's so unexpected. After confrontation, whether successful or not, the body often secretes slow releases of adrenalin in anticipation of consequence — comebacks. In door terms this might be police involvement, revenge attacks, mortality, etc.

Imagine the scenario: you've just given a guy a dig and someone approaches you and says, 'Do you know who that was? That's Joe Bloggs, he's connected'. WHOOSH! Or the police turn up, 'That man you hit an hour ago is in a coma, we think he might die'. FUCKING DOUBLE WHOOSH! (The police have said that to me even when it wasn't true, just to put the shits up me, and it worked.) Three guys in a city centre pub whacked my friend's brother with a duster and thought themselves pretty fucking tough until he arrived at the door of the pub an hour later and turned the place over.

Two of the doormen legged it out of the back and the other took a beasting. They all retired from the door that night because of the aftermath, but that still wasn't the end of the story for the two 'runners'. Two months later my friend caught up with them in the city centre one afternoon and placed them both in the care of the local hospital.

Two things you need to beat aftermath: 1) expect it to happen and tell yourself that when it does you'll handle it. 2) Make sure that you are 'in order' before you ever 'deal' with anyone. Justification is a very strong ally and you never know who you're dealing with. If I hit someone I don't care about aftermath because I will have made sure, in my own mind, that the deed needed doing. I never hit anyone unless I feel it is absolutely necessary, then if aftermath chases I won't run because karma is on my side and not theirs so they had better fucking watch out because there is no stronger, God given force.

'Adrenal combo' is what you get when you work the doors. Anyone working/living in a stress related environment, the stock exchange, business, security etc. may experience a combination (combo) of all former releases. Slow release, because you always anticipate confrontation; adrenal dump, when situations unexpectedly occur in your environment; and aftermath, in relation to situations that have already happened — you are always expecting situations to 'come back' on you.

Adrenal combo can have a dire effect on your personal life and for those doormen out there who are wondering why they are constantly tired and moody let me tell you that it's probably due to this syndrome. As I said before, train it off and try not to take it out on those closest to you. Just for your information — and I hope that I'm not boring you with all this, if I am don't hesitate to go to the next chapter — here are the expected physical reactions expected with adrenalin. The reason I am listing them is because they are the same physical traits that the uninitiated associate with cowardice. It's not cowardice, it's natural and needs to be understood and controlled (for those who haven't read my book on fear this is straight from there).

Adrenal reactions

Pre-fight shakes: your legs, and possibly other limbs, may shake uncontrollably. You have to learn to hide the 'shake' so that your opponent can't see it.

Dry mouth: your mouth may become dry and pasty. Have a coke or a glass of water.

Voice quiver: your voice may acquire a nervous and audible tremor. This also has to be hidden. The shaky voice says to anyone listening 'I'm scared'.

Tunnel vision: on the positive side tunnel vision enhances visual concentration. Its negative by product is blinkering of peripheral vision. Be aware of this and always keep your eye on the periphery. That's where the attack will likely come from.

Sweaty palms and forehead: the palms of the hands and forehead often sweat profusely. This is specially so if you are a fat bloke.

Nausea: adrenalin may cause vomiting, or the feeling of vomiting. The body does not need any excess baggage in fight or flight so un-digested food will be catapulted from your stomach. If you have notice of a fight don't eat anything heavy an hour before unless you want to see it again as a 'pavement pizza'.

Bowel loosening: the recipient may experience constant urges to use the toilet. It doesn't need digested food so will try an off-load that too. Pretty embarrassing if you are trying to play it cool and your bowels suddenly desert you on the pavement. This can be controlled: just tighten your bum and lock the feeling off. It's always wise to have an 'empty' before work. If you have notice of a fight go to the toilet and get rid of it.

'Yellow' fever: adrenalin, certainly adrenal dump, evokes feelings of helplessness and abject terror. Fear of confrontation may bring on an extreme feeling of depression and foreboding. Tears may also occur. Understanding that adrenalin/fear is natural will help you to captain these feelings, it is only ignorance that allows them to burgeon.

Time distortion: many people have reported — me being one of them — that confrontation seemed to last an eternity, when in reality it may have only lasted a few seconds. During confrontation time can appear to stand still, one minute often feeling like one hour. Paradoxically, in retrospect, many have said, 'It all happened so fast'. When interviewing James, the victim of an unsolicited assault, he initially told me that he was attacked without warning. After talking to him at some length it turned out that, between first seeing his attackers and the attack itself, there was a time lapse of eleven seconds, this being lost to time distortion. Memory loss and memory distortion are also common so what you say to the police in your statement might not be correct, even if you think it is at the time. Remember if you have to make a statement to the police, after the fact, you will be convicted for what you say and not what you have done. What you remember may be completely distorted due to adrenal exposure so refuse, if necessary, to make a statement until you have professional representation. The police, the little blighters, will try to insist that you make a statement there and then — I may have already said this somewhere in the book but it stands repeating — don't be bullied into it, you have rights.

Restless nights and no appetite: many suffer from restless nights when experiencing slow release and aftermath, and appetite tends to lessen, often resulting in weight loss, especially with slow release and aftermath. We spoke about this earlier, so feed yourself whether you are hungry or not and train away the un-utilised adrenalin for a good night's sleep.

Irrational behaviour can be due to constant exposure or over exposure to the adrenal syndrome, especially where adrenalin is released but not utilised. In the long term this is often the direct or indirect cause of temper tantrums, unprovoked violent outbursts, irrational behaviour, road rage, marriage breakdowns — the list goes on. Any of this sound familiar? It's like the story of my fucking life (oh yea, it is the story of my life!). It's all part of working the doors. So next time the guy at the bar says 'you've got a great job, you have,' tell him to fuck off and get a life.

What I want to get across in this chapter is that all of the foregoing feelings are usual. Accept them whenever possible: they are all part and parcel of life on the door and, though unpleasant, quite natural. These feelings do lessen in intensity as you become more exposed to them and they do become easier to control. So go and make the wife a cup of tea and apologise for all the times you were short with her, tell her why you were like it, give the kids a kiss and tell them too. These people are your life, the 'door' is only your job. And next time you feel like ripping their heads off go into the shed and hit the bag for half an hour or go for a long run. When you come back you won't want to shout at your lady you'll just want to give her a big hug — and maybe other things too. Now that you know about fear there is no reason to be so afraid of it, as Franklin D Roosevelt once said, 'The only thing we have to fear is fear itself'.

9. A Night Off!?

One thing in life is for sure and that is, when you work the door you need time away from all the confrontation and the violence. You have to have a break. Eventually the pressure builds up and if you don't take yourself away from the exposed environment you're bound to explode. It happened to me on a couple of occasions until I learned to spot the signs and 'pull myself away' before the pressure cooker blew its top. It's incredible how many people work the doors, or in any confrontational job like the police, security etc. and do not learn to listen to their own bodies. What usually occurs if you don't take control is that the pressure unleashes itself at the least expected time: at home, in the car, at Mcdonald's, anywhere. That's why you get road rage, or marriage breakdowns, unprovoked violent attacks etc. (Did we do this scenario already — I thinks so.)

The trouble is, as a doorman, it is very hard to have a night off without the phone ringing, or the door knocking or, when you go out, someone asking you to stop an argument. You're like an off duty policeman who is never really 'off duty'. In the late eighties I'd had my fill of confrontation with at least a fight a week — sometimes two in a night — for over four years and was pretty fucking desperate for a night away from the pressure. Chris, my friend, was having his little girl Christened and me and my then wife Nina were invited to the party. A great opportunity, I thought, to take a break, have a drink and be comfortable in the company of some nice, non-fighting people.

The party was being held at the local rugger club, which was basically just a two story building in the middle of a local rugger ground with a bar on the upper floor. Good, I thought, the further away from strangers the better. I was fed up with going to weddings and looking across the church aisle to see a guy that I had knocked out the week before. The party was going well and for the first time in about two years I was actually having Sunday night off the door. There were little kids running around everywhere: three of them were mine, and the families and friends of both Chris and his wife Val were having a ball. For the first time in I don't know how long I actually switched off and had a good drink. I am not a big drinker usually and I never had more than four halves of lager (and few bags of smoky bacon crisps of course) when I worked the door. A drunk doorman creates more trouble than he stops and, I knew, alcohol badly affects your timing, distancing, balance and perception. When they all go to pot you're about as much use as a chocolate fire guard.

That didn't matter tonight, I was in good company and there was absolutely no danger of trouble. These were all people that I knew and trusted — I thought.

Have you noticed, in life, that whenever a fight starts in a bar and someone is injured there is always some young thing who pushes through the crowd and says 'I'm a nurse!' and whenever two women have a fight there is always a stiletto shoe missing at the end of it all? Well the same goes with weddings, funerals and Christenings; whenever you attend one there is always one nob who spoils the fun for everyone else. At Chris's party the perfunctory nob was one of his own workmates who'd drunk enough to convince himself that he was the toughest fighter in the world, if not the universe, and a dashing Romeo.

When I went to the bar for a drink he was eyeing up every male as potential sparring partners and every female as likely bed mates. He was also holding a can of Breaker (beer) in each hand just to confirm to anyone interested that he could 'ave a drink'. Frankly my idea of prowess is not how many pints a man can get down his neck in one session. When people brag to me that they, or their mate, can drink twenty pints of lager and still walk home I find myself in yawn city and thinking 'what do you do for an encore, eat a pie shop?' It's a sad existence if your claim to fame is forcing your bladder to defy the laws of expansion by filling it with twenty pints of beer from the tap.

I noticed him as I went to the bar and ignored him again in the same breath. I'd seen a million nobs over the last eight years, just like this one, and was pleased that tonight it wasn't my job to deal with him if he 'kicked off'. I presumed that he was related to one of the families and I'm sure that they could better deal with him than I. It doesn't go down well, let me tell you, when you 'drop' the host's uncle, or brother at a family get together. I went back to my seat and carried on as though nothing had happened — nothing had so it was pretty easy.

As well as making you the best fighter in the world seven cans of Breaker also make you the best looking, most desirable bloke on the planet. 'The nob' looked in the toilet mirror and didn't see the reflection of man carrying 103% body fat — that's 1% more than Homer Simpson — he didn't see a spotty 'pizza' face that came with free garlic bread, neither did he see the ill-fitting suit with sweat stains under the armpits and cartoon smell lines at the crutch. What he did see in the 'magic mirror', and in his semi drunken stupor, was a super stud. In my opinion he had more chance of attracting flies than lovely ladies.

When he left the loo and tried to steal a 'smooch' from one of the young girls on the dance floor he couldn't believe his ears when she turned him down — she had obviously not looked in the same mirror as he — so, in his frustration he pushed her out of the way. The girl's father, not having any of that, gave the 'nob' a piece of his mind and the usual argument, bordering on a fight that would eventually and inevitably spoil the whole day, ensued.

I heard the cafuffle from where I sat in the corner talking to my good friend Pete but took no notice, that is until Val, Chris's wife, approached me at my table.

'Geoff, give us an 'and will ya? That dick'ead's gonna spoil the whole day. 'E's a right wanker but no one can control 'im.'

That's what I liked about Val, she had a lovely way with words. I couldn't say no, how could I? I let out a disappointed sigh, left the table and went to 'work'. I approached the debacle by the bar and the 'nob' was surrounded by several nice people who were all trying to get him to calm down. No chance, he was in his element and thriving on the attention. The more fuss they made of him the more aggressive he became. They were all trying to convince him that this wasn't the place to fight and that there were children and old people present. He didn't give a monkey's fuck and told them so.

I pushed through the melée and put my arm over the shoulder of the youth. He didn't deserve the nice approach but I didn't want to be fighting at a Christening of all places. I liked all of the people in here, Chris and Val's family were lovely people and I wanted to be respectful to them.

'Listen mate . . .' I said it really nice so as not to arouse the lad. 'Don't kick off in here, these are nice people, they don't want trouble. Look,' I pointed to all the children running around and the old people sitting watching, 'the place is full of kids and old people. They don't want this. Please — have a word with yourself.'

He looked right through me and then pushed me away. I felt the adrenalin rise and my anger pricked its ears. I held it back, this wasn't the right place for fighting. I stepped back in again, same approach, this time I dropped my chin low in case he hit me with the head. I lightly placed my left hand on his shoulder.

'There's no need for that mate, listen I'm just trying to . . .'

He pushed me again. That was twice too many.

WHACK!! I rammed my right hand around his throat and ran him backwards, smashing him through the exit doors that led to an iron grate staircase. He crashed through the doors and his back rammed into the iron handrail at the top of the stairs. I was right behind him and about ten people ran right behind me. I was just about to give the lad a firm telling off when he lunged forward at me.

BANG!!!! I instinctively dropped the head on him as he lunged and he dropped like a sack of shit. He was out there with Pluto. I looked at my feet to see where he had gone and he was sliding face-first down the iron staircase, whacking his teeth off every step with a sickly clang-clang-clang! I chased behind and caught him about half way down.

BOSH!!! I kicked him in the head and he finished his journey to the bottom. He was in sleepsville.

'That's for making me fight at my mate's Christening,' I shouted. He didn't listen. They never do when they're unconscious. Chris and all the other male guests followed me down like an entourage and I apologised profusely for the fight. They acknowledged that I only did what they all wanted to do and thanked me for getting rid of him.

'YOU BLOODY ANIMAL!! YOU BASTARD! YOU BULLY!'

Hello, I thought, not everyone's happy. It was one of Val's neighbours. She looked just like 'Miss Piggy', though not quite so nice looking. Her make-up was heavy, like it had been put on with a bricklayer's trowel. The metal stairs trembled under her feet as she bounded down towards us and her jowled face shuddered with each step she took. These stairs just weren't made for that kind of punishment. We all stood in awe and stared, silently placing bets as to whether or not the staircase would collapse under her weight — I hoped they might — or whether in fact she might put the earth's centre of gravity out of plum when she hit terra firma.

She had 'Sumo' thighs: they were huge. No wonder her husband had two cauliflower ears, and her fat arse dragged behind her like a wedding trail. I remember thinking, 'Fuck me, it's Bodicea'. Her lipstick was thick and uneven like she'd put it on during a sneezing fit. She'd apparently witnessed the very end of the scenario with me and the 'nob' and, as is often the case, got the wrong end of the stick. She barged past me and made a bee-line for the 'poor boy' that I had 'so brutally beaten up for no reason'. I have to say that she was an ugly cow and had she been a man — she could quite easily have passed for one — I'd have given her a slap as well.

'YOU'RE JUST A BULLY! ANY EXCUSE FOR A FIGHT. YOU CAN SEE THAT THIS IS JUST A NICE LAD WHO WOULDN'T HURT A FLY. LOOK AT HIM, HE'S A LOVELY LAD. NOT A BAD WORD FROM HIM. YOU'RE JUST A BULLY!'

Her husband, a nice bloke who couldn't be blamed for the things she was saying to me, meekly followed behind her like Kermit the Frog. He looked at me and shrugged his big shoulders.

'Sorry Geoff. You know what she's like!'

I did know, I was just glad that I didn't have to sleep with her. She approached the lad and put her arm around him.

'You alright love?'

'Fuck off you ugly fat cow!' he said, and pushed her away.

Well, there you go, I obviously misjudged the lad. Maybe he wasn't so bad after all? I could have cried laughing as she ran back into the club blarting. Her husband hesitated for a second, unsure whether to hit the lad or buy him a drink. She stopped on the stairs and gave him a glare that said 'the former', so he jumped on the 'nob' to defend her honour. It was a pretty half-hearted attempt that stopped as soon as she disappeared out of sight.

I went back into the club to finish my drink and did my best to forget the debacle that was supposed to be my night off. The lads outside convinced the 'nob' to 'go home whilst you still have some teeth in your head'. He took their advice and left for the safety of another bar, any bar that I wasn't sitting in. So much for a rest.

At work the next day the 'nob' complained to Chris about me knocking his teeth out. Chris rang me to let me know that his mate wasn't happy and I told him that I'd gladly meet the lad 'any time, any place' and knock the rest of them out for him. He never took me up on the offer and Chris's neighbour, 'Miss Piggy', never spoke to me again — so at least some good came out of the situation.

10. Last night on the door — the end of an era.

When I started the door I was frightened of my own shadow and confrontation seemed an ugly and unapproachable monster. Now, nine years on, I sported broken knuckles, the perfunctory broken nose, a cauliflower ear and enough scars on my head and body to warrant a personal grid reference and the confidence of ten men. My life had completely turned around for the better. I had, as they say, arrived. I had finished my apprenticeship. I had gone from being frightened of fighting to being a fighter of repute with over three hundred battles lying in my wake and to my credit.

Sounds a lot, I know. It might even sound as though I made it up but in reality three hundred wasn't and isn't that many in a city that was full of people who wanted to fight, for any reason, even though most of them couldn't fight tiredness.

I had some amazing times on the door and made some absolutely wonderful friends who I had grown to love, admire and respect. I consider myself the luckiest man alive to have been exposed to these larger than life characters who guided and influenced me in a way that I still cannot believe. It sounds like a fairy story when a man can go from the bottom of the heap of the top of the castle in one lifetime but that's what I did and I am grateful to have 'survived the journey', basically intact. It would be easy at this point to glamourise the whole scenario by telling of great friends and exciting adventures but I can't and mustn't forget the adversity, the times when I couldn't sleep for fear of incarceration, comebacks, killing, being killed, maiming, being maimed, and I can't forget also the profound personal changes that I had to go through to metamorphose into the man I am today.

Yes, I made it, but at what cost? The price, I have to say, was high — though I'd gladly have paid twice the amount because every bit of pain, of blood and snot, of fear, of threat, of persecution and of sacrifice was worth it.

At 36 I feel as though I have already lived two lifetimes. When I left the door it was as a dauntless man who feared no confrontation too much to meet it. I had faced down many fearful men and destroyed my own demons like weeds in the garden. I had pushed my own physical and mental boundaries until I thought I might fall dead, and then pushed some more. Along the way I was forced to be so violent that, at times, I no longer recognised who I was, or at least who I had become. People told me that I had changed, some said for the better, others, for the worst. Even my mum, who I love dearly, said that I had become 'hard' and had lost the tenderness of her 'Geoffrey' — she was right. But I couldn't see it at the time. I was too close.

That was until I sat down one day, long after I had finished the doors, and re-read *Watch My Back*. What a shock! I remember thinking, 'Was that really me, did I do all those terrible things to other human beings?' Was it justified, was I over the top, was I, quote, 'a fucking hair trigger?' Being honest I had to admit that yes I was many of those things and probably more, I put my hands up to it, but when you work the doors in a city like Coventry they are the vital prerequisites to entering and certainly surviving the job. In this trade you had to be first because there were the quick and then there were the dead. I didn't want to fall into the latter category. If I did it all again I wouldn't change a thing because anything less and I'd have been picked out and fucked like a free whore in the only brothel in town.

Then there was the pressure. That might not be fully appreciated for the outside looking in, like the guy at the Navigation pub where I worked and encountered some major violence (stories in *Watch My Back* & *Bouncer*). At the beginning of the night he came into the pub to find me reclined on a garden chair at the front entrance to the pub eating a bag of smoky bacon crisps and drinking a half a lager. He told me that I had the best job in the world. And he believed it, too. Half an hour later we had a visit for the local heavies and Tony and I tore them new arseholes. Within twenty minutes of the beating the whole pub was smashed up by their gang and we had threats on our lives coming out of the woodwork. The same guy who had said our job was heaven left the pub (he was allowed to go home, we had to stay). On his exit he looked at me and said, 'I wouldn't be in your shoes for a million pounds'. That guy received enlightenment inside one hour.

Sometimes the job is great, other times you hate it with a passion. At times the pressure upon me, and every doorman, was tremendous but, with the benefit of hindsight, I can see that the pressures — and subsequently handling them — are responsible for what and who I am today. They were there for many reasons.

The punishing adversity of doorwork allowed me to see who I was and what I had to offer. Its employment also separated the wheat from the chaff. Whilst the weak of will and faint of heart crumbled under the onslaught of violence and its threat, it also strengthened the wills and hearts of those who stayed the course. Working the doors, putting myself under that extreme pressure, was like immersing an inner-tube into a bowl of water and applying air pressure to find out where the leaks were. When the bubbles rose and the inner-tube lifted out of the water the holes were ear marked for inspection and then systematically sealed up. The door was my metaphoric bowl of water. The bad people in society applied the pressure, and time and training sealed my leaks, and the leaks of anyone who endured.

The mental demands of such taxing pressure develops strong minds in those who don't give in. At the same time it can destroy those who can't handle the pace. The pressure was injected from every angle and in varying disguises. If you had a weakness it would be found, dragged out into the open and then poked with insulting, personal and often outrageous insults, until you either stopped caring or you threw in the towel.

If you didn't like racism you became a 'fucking nigger lover' and got 'black jibes' till they came out of your ears. If you didn't like being bawled at, you got it until your ear drums ached. If you were receding you became 'fucking slap head', fat, you were 'gut bucket', Welsh, 'Taffy bastard', Scots, 'Jock strap' and Irish, 'thick paddy bastard!' If you didn't like being poked, pushed, pulled, bullied, baited, laughed about, spat at or pissed on, whatever it was you didn't like you got in bags full. And if the punters didn't do it to you then the other doormen would, in an innate form of initiation that prepared those who endured and destroyed those who baulked. Cruel but kind.

John was the master of it and in my time at Buster's the bird threw me from pillar to post and strangled me every time we had a quiet moment. To those watching it would seem cruel and unnecessary but they were the uninitiated and knew no better. Being thrown around by John and being ripped to bits with scathing sarcasm by the other lads was no different to a tiger being heavy with its cub to prepare it for a sticky jungle. It was hard at times but imperative to survival. Pressure opens up character flaws that allow the enemy to see right through you, like a personality X-Ray. Personal stress fractures can be mended and strengthened, but not until they have been located. So if the punters didn't do it then the other doormen would. They did it because they cared, it was part of the training. If they didn't do it you wouldn't survive. It was that simple.

So, the door was my locating arena. Only at the time I didn't know this, it was an unspoken, even subliminal truth and I was left to work it out for myself. Not every doorman found this enlightenment; I did and it was a revelation. The ones that didn't threw in the towel believing the world unjust, sadistic and unfair — a pretty fair description. So I paid the price, mentally and physically, but if you want to see the diamond you have to crack away the rock.

When I finally decided to leave the door it was because in the end, and like most people who work this trade, I grew to hate it. When I first started the door I was an unhappy man in an unhappy marriage and I felt that the risks were worth the rewards. With one broken marriage behind me — when I said broken I meant smashed to fucking pieces — and a new lady who meant more to me than life, the risks started outweighing the rewards. And I suppose without wanting to sound pretentious and 'know it all' I had learned what I had come to learn and hanging around waiting for the inevitable knife in the back or spell in jail seemed futile.

I had also grown sick of the 'fight mentality' of the punters that I was dealing with. Most of them were absolute wankers who wanted to insult and debase you then fucking run like school children to the police when you split their lip — I mean, what's the world coming to when you can't have a fight without some nob getting you arrested? And these people think they're tough — they couldn't fucking spell it. In short, I lost my faith in human nature.

Watch My Back had been released for about 6 months and had caused quite a stir in the city. A lot of the people that I wrote about, the ones that I had fought least ways, were not happy about my derogatory descriptions of them and they made a few aggressive noises. This surprised me somewhat because most of them are thicker than a whale omelette and I was sure they wouldn't recognise themselves without accompanying photos and arrows that said 'this is you, you thick bastard'. I thought they were illiterate — maybe they got their probation officers to read it to them. All the same they were not HP. When I went to visit them to sort the problem out they no longer seemed so keen to complain, a sudden change of heart, there's a surprise — so I made it clear in that book as I do in this that if the people I have fought were/are not happy about what I have to say then give me a call and I'll mark out an arena at the local park for a straightener. No seconds, no spectators, just me and you — then I'll do my very best to maim you in any way I can. That's my game! That's what I do, it's what I train every day of my life for. One fight CAN change the course of your life, don't let anyone tell you that it can't.

With the book out and TV interviews about the 'bouncer who wrote a book' — what a novelty — the door had become difficult for me to work, it was like being in a fucking fish bowl. People were constantly asking me about the book and watching my every move like a hawk to see if I could really 'go'. One young girl actually approached me one night and said frankly,

'What do I have to do to get into your book?'

'You have to either fight me or shag me,' I said laughing.

Sharon, who was stood next to me said with a wry smile, 'Well I've done both and I'm not in it?'

So the door was becoming a bit of a bind. *Watch My Back* was doing well and I didn't need the money any more, either. I had always said that once things were better financially I'd drop the door and try to make my living writing. Funny enough I mentioned this to a friend — some friend — and he all but scoffed. 'Who did I think I was?' Well, if he is reading this, now I do make my fucking living from writing, and that's thanks to all the lovely people out their who did not scoff and who follow my books. Thank you very much for the support. You can do anything if you believe in yourself and don't let negative people drag you down.

So now I didn't need the money I had nothing stopping me, yet I still couldn't bring myself to leave the trade that had been my life for the better part of a decade. I spoke to Ian on the phone and he asked me why I was still working when I didn't need to. I couldn't answer. Maybe I thought my friends would think I was selling out. 'Not if they are real friends,' Ian said. I spoke to Sharon. She had wanted me to leave the door for some time but didn't want to push me, 'it has to be your own decision'. I spoke to my mum and dad, they'd wanted me to leave for years and were over the moon that I was even thinking about it. You don't realise at the time but working in a violent environment affects a lot of people around you, especially the people who love you. I decided to leave.

My last night was set for the Monday at the Devon pub where I had spent the last three years under the head doormanship of a legend, Seymore. All the lads took the news well and wished me the best of luck. They didn't take it too seriously, I don't think, because most doormen are always 'leaving the door for good this time' and do so at least once a year. Tony 'the head' used to retire about ten times a year. So I suppose the lads didn't really take my retirement seriously and didn't think I'd be gone for long so there was no sense in making too much of a fuss. I guess that's why they didn't give me a send off party or a card or anything official to say 'so long'. I understood that.

Driving home knowing that I never had to go back again was like lifting a lead weight off my shoulders, I felt as light as a feather. I also felt sad. A thousand memories drifted into my head as I broke through the darkness in my Sierra and purred along the empty streets to my home. Memories floated in like old friends: being so scared that I wanted to die, my first night at Buster's, my first KO, throwing the ugliest women in the world out of Buster's and laughing till I cried when she attacked the doors with a shoe, Awesome Anderson, No-neck Maynard, Jabber James, kissing the beautiful KT on the dance floor and falling in love with her only to see her flee the club never to come back into my life again, the lady in red who enchanted me, the nurse who mummied me, the beautiful half caste girl who asked to take me to bed, knocking out five men with a duster, being in a police cell all night as a consequence, getting off without charge, a doorman's estranged wife who asked me to shag her to get back at him, saving the police women at the rave, the gorgeous nurse who got glassed, me getting glassed, putting Mr S on hospital food, getting divorced, crying for my children, living in a bedsit, moving in with Sharon, nearly killing the Karate kid, bashing Mr G, writing *Watch My Back*, leaving the door, no longer feeling scared anymore.

So what did I learn from facing danger as a way of life and having to fight my way to enlightenment? What I learned and what I know is this: there are no archetypal, fearless heroes with chilled water for blood and asbestos for skin; no robotic, emotionless killing machines with 'Action Man' haircuts and balls of steel. We are all flesh and blood, men with mothers and fathers who love us, wives and children who depend upon us. We all feel apprehension with anticipation, fear with confrontation and stress and frustration with aftermath. The great Cus Damatio, trainer to Mike Tyson, said that the coward and the hero both feel the same feelings, the difference is the hero handles them and the coward does not.

I have to say that many times I felt like a coward, only my decision to go forward deemed me, for want of a better word, a hero. Within even the bravest of people there is a coward just bursting to get out. After a lifetime's searching I found no tangible nirvana, only enlightenment; no metaphoric pot of gold at the end of the rainbow, rather, the experience and information collected en route. Neither did I gain the mystic cloak I thought came with being a 'bouncer', only knowledge. Enlightenment allowed me a three hundred and sixty degree look at myself, warts and all; experience gave me the reference points and information to work from when situations got ugly. And knowledge? An understanding of my own bodily reactions to confrontation and adversity, identifying fear as an ally, 'the friend of exceptional people', whilst at the same time recognising that un-contained fear was the mind killer.

At the end of my search I realised what General Sun Tzu had voiced some twenty five centuries earlier, that understanding your enemy and understanding yourself did indeed allow you to face a hundred battles without fear of defeat. Confrontation and good training spurned positive and spontaneous decision making, this often being called bravery. Through this, victory could be calculated. Any man that can stand the heat of adversity can mould himself into anything or anyone he desires: a weak person may become strong, a soft person hard. It had been a long journey, I had come a long way, I was tired but very happy. My tour of duty was over, a new life lay a head. Would I do it all again? You bet your fucking house I would.

Epilogue

Writing the bouncer books has been great fun for me, troublesome at times because of having to re-live some of the more traumatic times of my life, but still fun. I am so very flattered that people have bought my books and have been kind enough to support me in my endeavour to make a better life for myself. Writing the books has enabled me to meet some great people all over the country and the world. I feel privileged. I would just like to take this opportunity once again to thank you all for your support and I hope you enjoyed the stories.

Best of respect — Geoff Thompson, Coventry, 1996.